AN AGE OF SCIENCE AND REVOLUTIONS, 1600–1800 FILMS AND DOCUMENTARIES

There is a large body of work available in DVD and VHS format relating to this period in time. The following films may be useful to you in this unit:

Amistad (1997). Steven Spielberg's film is about a mutiny in 1839 on board a slave ship traveling toward the northeast coast of America. Much of the story involves a courtroom drama about the slave who led the revolt.

The Declaration of Independence (Goldhill Video, "Just the Facts" learning series, 2000). This documentary explores the political forces that existed before 1776 and the socioeconomic realities that made it necessary to declare to the world our independence from Great Britain. It examines the body of knowledge that contributed to the Declaration of Indepence, including the Magna Carta of 1215.

Galileo: On the Shoulders of Giants (1998). Directed by David Devine, this video is part of the *Inventors' Specials*, an award-winning series of programs for children, introducing them to some of the world's leading scientists and inventors. Presented in fictionalized fashion, the account focuses on the relationship between the great astronomer Galileo and his apprentice, Cosimo de Medici II, Grand Duke of Tuscany.

Galileo's Battle for the Heavens (PBS, 2002). This documentary offers a comprehensive look at Galileo Galilei's contributions to science in the midst of a turbulent era. PBS also has a useful companion website (including articles, timelines, and other educational resources) to this film: www.pbs.org/wgbh/nova/galileo.

The Great Wall of China (The History Channel, "Modern Marvels" series). Available on DVD and VHS, this documentary explores the construction of the Great Wall and examines the mysteries of one of the most awe-inspiring monuments in the world.

Guns of the Orient (The History Channel, "Tales of the Gun" series). Available on VHS, this documentary is an eye-opening look at the incredible, exotic weapons produced in places like China, Turkey and India.

The Jewel in the Crown (8-volume set). Available on DVD and VHS, this adaptation of Paul Scott's masterpiece, *The Raj Quartet*, won more than 20 international awards, including a Golden Globe and an Emmy. Filmed on location, it re-creates the turbulent period when British colonial rule in India came crashing down. Students should find this story interesting after reading about the beginnings of colonial rule in India.

Newton: A Tale of Two Isaacs (1997). Directed by Don McBrearty. The story of Isaac Newton and his revolutionary scientific theories are the subject of this video production, which is part of the *Inventors' Specials* series. Among the stated goals of the show is that of instilling values of hard work and perseverance. The story is a fictionalized account of the adventures of Newton and his assistant, as they work against resistance from the scientific community and public to Newton's research. Filmed in Ireland, with authentic period costumes, the production reenacts famous incidents, including the apple experiment and Newton's presentation of his gravitational theory before London's Royal Society.

A Passage to India (1984). Although the film takes place in the 1920s, this story introduces some interesting ideas about the tension between Indians and the colonial British—a relationship which grew out of the British East India Company. This film is based on E. M. Forster's novel of the same title.

Sir Isaac Newton: The Gravity of Genius (A&E Home Video, 1996). This documentary about Isaac Newton originally was broadcast on the television series *Biography* in 1995 and is now available on VHS.

The SuperStar Teachers Series: The Origin of the Modern Mind and *The Great Minds of the Western Intellectual Tradition* (The Teaching Company; 1991, 1993). This set of educational films offers a series of lessons from professors on the origins of modern scientific thought, traced through the work of Descartes, Bacon and Newton.

An Age of Science and Revolutions 1600–1800

Teaching Guide

Oxford University Press, Inc., publishes works that
further Oxford University's objective of excellence
in research, scholarship, and education.

Oxford   New York
Auckland   Cape Town   Dar es Salaam   Hong Kong   Karachi
Kuala Lumpur   Madrid   Melbourne   Mexico City   Nairobi
New Delhi   Shanghai   Taipei   Toronto

With offices in
Argentina   Austria   Brazil   Chile   Czech Republic   France   Greece
Guatemala   Hungary   Italy   Japan   Poland   Portugal   Singapore
South Korea   Switzerland   Thailand   Turkey   Ukraine   Vietnam

Copyright © 2005 by Oxford University Press, Inc.

Published by Oxford University Press, Inc.
198 Madison Avenue, New York, NY, 10016
www.oup.com

Oxford is a registered trademark of Oxford University Press

All rights reserved. No part of this publication may be reproduced,
stored in a retrieval system, or transmitted, in any form or by any means,
electronic, mechanical, photocopying, recording, or otherwise,
without the prior permission of Oxford University Press.

ISBN-13: 978-0-19-522255-5 (California edition)   ISBN-13: 978-0-19-522346-0

Writer: Sara Jo Schwartz
Manuscript Development: Morrison BookWorks, LLD
Project Director: Jacqueline A. Ball
Education Consultant: Diane L. Brooks, Ed.D.
Design: designlabnyc

Casper Grathwohl, Publisher

Printed in the United States of America
on acid-free paper

CONTENTS

Note to the Teacher	5
The Medieval & Early Modern World Program Using the Teaching Guide and Student Study Guide	6
Improving Literacy with *The Medieval & Early Modern World*	16
Group Projects	20

Teaching Strategies for *An Age of Science and Revolutions, 1600–1800*

Chapter 1	Settlements, Trade and Conflict: The North American Experience	26
Chapter 2	Rude Awakenings: Wealth Redefined	32
Chapter 3	Most Magnificent: The Ottoman Empire	38
Chapter 4	Peacocks and the Power of Pachyderms: The Wonders of Mughal India	44
Chapter 5	Missionaries, Maps, and Magistrates With Pink Parasols: China Encounters Modern Science	50
Chapter 6	The Secrets of the Heavens: New Scientific Theories	56
Chapter 7	The Toolbox of the Enlightenment: The Scientific Revolution	62
Chapter 8	Bold Ideas and Prison Sentences: The Literary Life	68
Chapter 9	Rising Stars: Women in the Enlightenment	74
Chapter 10	Heads Rolling: Democracy and the Consent of the People	80

Wrap-Up Test	86
Rubrics	88
Graphic Organizers	92
Answer Key (Teaching Guide and Student Study Guide)	100

HISTORY FROM OXFORD UNIVERSITY PRESS

"A thoroughly researched political and cultural history... makes for a solid resource for any collection."
– School Library Journal

THE WORLD IN ANCIENT TIMES
RONALD MELLOR AND AMANDA H. PODANY, EDS.
THE EARLY HUMAN WORLD
THE ANCIENT NEAR EASTERN WORLD
THE ANCIENT EGYPTIAN WORLD
THE ANCIENT SOUTH ASIAN WORLD
THE ANCIENT CHINESE WORLD
THE ANCIENT GREEK WORLD
THE ANCIENT ROMAN WORLD
THE ANCIENT AMERICAN WORLD

"Bringing history out of the Dark Ages!"

THE MEDIEVAL AND EARLY MODERN WORLD
BONNIE G. SMITH, ED.
THE EUROPEAN WORLD, 400-1450
THE AFRICAN AND MIDDLE EASTERN WORLD, 600-1500
THE ASIAN WORLD, 600-1500
AN AGE OF EMPIRES, 1200-1750
AN AGE OF VOYAGES, 1350-1600
AN AGE OF SCIENCE AND REVOLUTIONS, 1600-1800

"The liveliest, most realistic, most well-received American history series ever written for children."
– Los Angeles Times

A HISTORY OF US
JOY HAKIM
THE FIRST AMERICANS
MAKING THIRTEEEN COLONIES
FROM COLONIES TO COUNTRY
THE NEW NATION
LIBERTY FOR ALL?
WAR, TERRIBLE WAR
RECONSTRUCTING AMERICA
AN AGE OF EXTREMES
WAR, PEACE, AND ALL THAT JAZZ
ALL THE PEOPLE

FOR MORE INFORMATION, VISIT US AT WWW.OUP.COM

New from Oxford University Press
Reading History, by Janet Allen
ISBN 0-19-516595-0 hc 0-19-516596-9 pb

"*Reading History* is a great idea. I highly recommend this book."
–Dennis Denenberg, *Professor of Elementary and Early Childhood Education, Millersville University*

NOTE TO THE TEACHER

Dear Fellow Educator:

How do we realize our hopes and dreams? How do we face the challenges of everyday life? Everyone—old and young alike—asks such questions at one time or another. One place to look for answers is in the lives of people in the past. In history we find ordinary people building cathedrals and mosques, conducting trade over thousands of miles, eking out a living through agriculture and crafts, and dreaming dreams of creating vast empires. This series brings you their stories.

As educators, we want to present these stories as part of a living past—and the authors of our books aim to provide you with the materials to do just that. We offer ways to make the past come alive with vivid images in full color, lively accounts of actual people, and maps to show young readers where these people lived and how they traveled the world. Heroes tell us in their own words of their noblest hopes; villains show us their cruelty. Ordinary folks face the plague and young boys set out in creaky ships on dangerous seas. This series helps you show young adults the fullness of the past and the grand achievements that make up our heritage.

We all know that our task does not stop at presenting the *story* of the past. We must also teach our students the *skills* vital to understanding history and to becoming informed citizens. These books are designed to help you train students to think critically about human opinions, prejudices, and programs for the future. The many voices from historical actors in the series provide opportunities for students to come to terms with burning issues of bias and point of view.

You and I share not only great hopes for the future but also the daily challenges of teaching. In addition to the stories, images, quotes, maps, timelines, and young adult bibliographies of the books themselves, the series includes instructional guides with tested ideas for teaching the medieval and early modern world. These guides are filled with exercises, classroom activities, and daily lessons based on specific chapters in each book. They show additional, practical ways to make critical thinking an integral part of your work in world history.

The authors of the student books and the supporting instructional materials bring you and your students the very latest thinking about what world history is. We urge you to tell us how their presentation of this vital, emerging field works with your students. Good history, like the creation of civilization itself, depends on our common effort!

Bonnie G. Smith
General Editor

THE MEDIEVAL & EARLY MODERN WORLD PROGRAM

I. STUDENT EDITION

- Engaging, friendly narrative
- A wide range of primary sources in every chapter
- The authority of Oxford scholarship
- Period illustrations and specially commissioned maps

II. TEACHING GUIDE

- Wide range of activities and classroom approaches
- Strategies for universal access and improving literacy (ELL, struggling readers, advanced learners)
- Multiple assessment tools

III. STUDENT STUDY GUIDE

- Exercises correlated to Student Edition and Teaching Guide
- Portfolio approach
- Activities for every level of learning
- Literacy through reading and writing

PRIMARY SOURCES AND REFERENCE VOLUME

- Broad selection of primary sources in each subject area
- Ideal resource for in-class exercises and unit projects

TEACHING GUIDE: KEY FEATURES

The Teaching Guides organize each *Medieval & Early Modern World* book into chapter-based lessons of six (6) pages each, preceded by a special section that includes one longer-term project per chapter. These projects are cross-curricular, designed for mixed-group participation, and suitable for a wide range of learning styles. They can be used for teacher and student self- or peer assessment with the rubrics at the back of this Teaching Guide.

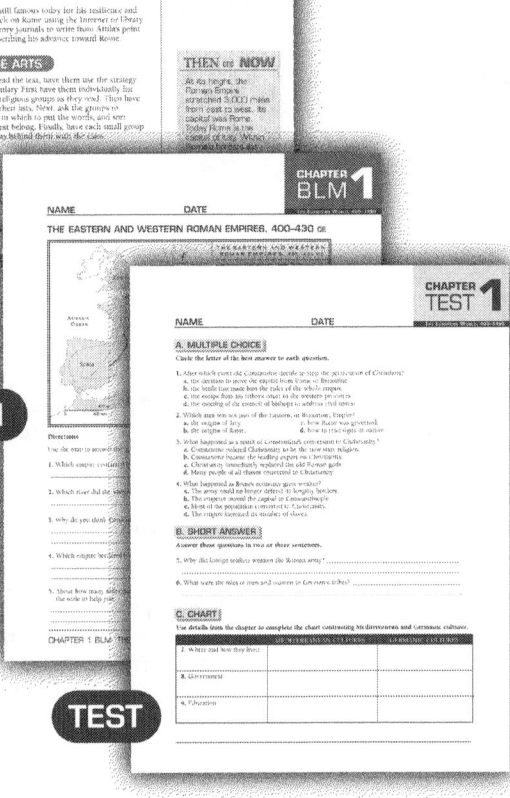

GROUP PROJECTS
Engaging, creative projects for group work on a wide variety of inviting topics

CHAPTER LESSONS
Teaching strategies and suggestions that address curriculum and that link with Student Study Guide and Student Edition

TESTS AND BLACKLINE MASTERS (BLMS)
Reproducible tests; map skills, primary sources, and document-based questions (DBQs) for assessment, homework, or classroom projects

TEACHING GUIDE: CHAPTER LESSONS

Teaching guides are organized so that you can easily find the information you need.

CHAPTER SUMMARY AND PERFORMANCE OBJECTIVES
The Chapter Summary gives an overview of the information in the chapter. The Performance Objectives are the three or four important goals students should achieve in the chapter. Accomplishing these goals will help students master the information in the book as well as meet standards for the course.

BUILDING BACKGROUND
This section connects students to the chapter they are about to read. Students may be asked to use what they know to make predictions about the text, preview the images in the chapter, or connect modern life with the historical subject matter.

VOCABULARY
A word list for every chapter defines difficult words and key curricular terms and recaps glossary entries.

CHAPTER 1

BELIEVERS AND BARBARIANS: THE END OF THE ROMAN EMPIRE
PAGES 20–33

FOR HOMEWORK
Student Study Guide pages 13–16
Chapter 1

CHAPTER SUMMARY
Both external and internal problems weakened Rome. When Constantine the Great converted to Christianity he moved the capital east to a city later renamed Constantinople. The empire gradually divided into the Eastern Empire and the Western Empire, each with its own version of Christianity. In 410 the Visigoths conquered Rome. However, Rome's legacy lived on through Latin, government structures, and architecture.

PERFORMANCE OBJECTIVES
▶ To identify the factors that threatened the Roman Empire
▶ To define and evaluate the key events in the life and rule of Constantine
▶ To identify the lasting contributions of Rome

BUILDING BACKGROUND
Ask students to preview the chapter by reading the headings and subheadings, studying the photographs and captions, and examining the map. Based on the preview, work with students to compile a list of questions about the fall of Rome and the rise of Christianity. As students locate the answers to their questions, have them record them on the list.

VOCABULARY
empire huge region of varied cultures under the control of one government
citizen person owing loyalty to and entitled to protection by a state or a nation
Christianity the religion based on the life and teachings of Jesus Christ
convert person who has been convinced to change from one religion to another
barbarian name given to outsiders by the Romans, who viewed them as uncivilized
drought a long period of very low rainfall
As needed, have students consult the glossary to define the following words: *bishop, centralize, council, excommunicate, heretic, New Testament, persecution, plunder, saint*

CAST OF CHARACTERS
Augustine (aw-GUS-teen), Roman nobleman who converted to Christianity
Constantine the Great (KON-stun-teen), First Roman emperor to convert to Christianity
Visigoths (VIH-zih-goths), Arian Christian Germanic tribe that attacked Rome in 410

WORKING WITH PRIMARY SOURCES
Point out the quotation from Ambrose in Student Edition page 23. If necessary, refer students to the glossary, and explain that excommunicated means to be deprived of the right of church membership by the church leadership. Discuss what the quotation reveals about early Christian beliefs. Why do you think Ambrose asked the emperor to repent? Invite students to read more of Ambrose's letter to the emperor, written in 390, at http://www.fordham.edu/halsall/source/ambrose-let51.html.

28 CHAPTER 1

WORKING WITH PRIMARY SOURCES
A major feature of *The Medieval & Early Modern World* is the opportunity to read about history through the words and images of the people who lived it. Each book includes excerpts from the best sources from these ancient civilizations, giving the narrative an immediacy that is difficult to match in secondary sources. Students can read further in these sources on their own or in small groups using the accompanying *Primary Sources and Reference Volume*. The Teaching Guide recommends activities so students of all skill levels can appreciate the ways people from the past saw themselves, their ideas and values, and their fears and dreams.

8

LINKING DISCIPLINES

Art Have students research examples of arches, roads, and aqueducts constructed throughout the Roman Empire. You might want to display a map of the Roman Empire on the wall. Instruct students to research in a library or on the Internet to find examples of Roman architecture. Have them sketch or print copies, write brief captions, and affix them on the map. Ask students to identify similarities between these ancient structures and familiar modern structures.

LITERACY TIPS

In addition to using the suggestions in the Supporting Learning and Extending Learning sections, refer back frequently to pages 20–23 for strategies and advice from a literacy coach.

WRITING

Persuasive Letter Have students review the events of Augustine's life as described in the chapter. Next have them write a persuasive letter or sermon that he might have addressed to non-Christians to describe his conversion and persuade them of his beliefs. What figurative language might he use to compel them? What experiences would he share from his life? *(Assessment: students incorporate supporting detail and language from the chapter. Their letters should also represent the tensions between Christians and non-Christians.)*

SUPPORTING LEARNING

English Language Learners Help students recognize and use multiple meaning words. Using the paragraphs on Student Edition page 27, identify and define such words as letters, beat, torn, and passage. Help students use context clues and their prior knowledge to figure out which meaning is being used. Ask volunteers to suggest sentences using various meanings of the words.

Struggling Readers Have students complete the Sequence of Events Chart at the back of the guide to show how one event led to another, and then another in the history of early Christianity. For example, they can list how Christianity's spread led to the executions of Christians, and so on. Remind them to look for key dates, such as Constantine's conversion in 312.

EXTENDING LEARNING

Enrichment Invite students to learn more about one of these cities as they are today: Rome, Carthage, or Constantinople. Direct students to use search engines...

GEOGRAPHY CONNECTION

Movement Have students trace the routes of the Germanic migrations on the map on page 31. They may want to compare the map with a topographic map of Europe to locate features, such as mountains or rivers that either blocked or aided the movement of these peoples.

READING COMPREHENSION QUESTIONS

1. Why did economic and social conditions worsen in Rome? *(Rome depended on slaves to produce food. When the empire stopped expanding, it had fewer slaves to do the work.)*
2. Why did Roman authorities fear the early Christians? *(They worried about uprisings. Christianity was becoming popular among people who would likely rebel: the poor in cities, slaves, and soldiers.)*
3. Where did Constantine locate the new capital of the empire? *(Byzantium, a small Greek city near Asia Minor)*
4. Why did the Huns migrate west? *(Drought ruined their pasture, and they wanted better lives for themselves.)*
5. What happened after the Visigoths advanced on Rome in 410? *(The western emperor fled, and the Visigoths plundered Rome.)*

CRITICAL THINKING QUESTIONS

1. What does the image of the shield on Student Edition page 23 tell you about warfare during this time? *(Warfare included hand-to-hand combat. Soldiers had access to iron for added protection.)*
2. Why were the Romans, Germanic tribes, and Huns in conflict with each other? *(They wanted to either keep control of land and resources, or gain land and resources from the other groups. They fought rather than cooperate with each other.)*
3. One Goth observer described the Huns as "small, foul, and skinny." What does it say about the Goths' view of the Huns during this time? *(It shows their negative opinion of the Goths.)*

SOCIAL SCIENCES

Military History Attila the Hun is still famous today for his resilience and brutality. Have students research his attack on Rome using the Internet or library resources. Next have them use their history journals to write from Attila's point of view a series of short diary entries describing his advance toward Rome.

READING AND LANGUAGE ARTS

Reading Nonfiction As students read the text, have them use the strategy "list/group/label" to work with the vocabulary. First have them individually list words that relate to different cultures or religious groups as they read. Then have students form groups of three and share their lists. Next, ask the groups to identify and name at least five categories in which to put the words, and sort them into the categories to which they best belong. Finally, have each small group display their choices and share the reasons behind them with the class.

Using Language Direct students' attention to the quotation from Ambrose on page 27. Have them draw in their history journals an image it brings to mind. With partners, students can share images and discuss why Ambrose might have described the church the way he did. Next, have partners consider what the "raging sea" represents. As a whole class, speculate about the effect of his words on both Christians and on non-Christians.

THE EUROPEAN WORLD, 400–1450   29

WRITING
Each chapter has a suggestion for a specific writing assignment. These assignments can help students meet state requirements in writing as well improve their skills.

SUPPORTING LEARNING AND EXTENDING LEARNING
Suggestions for students of varying abilities and learning styles: advanced learners, struggling readers, auditory/visual/tactile learners, and English language learners. These may be individual, partner, or group activities. *(For more on reading and literacy, see pp. 16–19.)*

GEOGRAPHY CONNECTION
Each chapter has a Geography Connection to strengthen students' map skills as well as their understanding of how geography affects human civilization. One of the five themes of geography is highlighted in each chapter.

READING COMPREHENSION AND CRITICAL THINKING QUESTIONS
The reading comprehension questions are general enough to allow free-flowing class or small group discussion, yet specific enough to be used for oral or written assessment of students' grasp of the important information. The critical thinking questions are intended to engage students in a deeper analysis of the text and can also be used for oral or written assessment.

SOCIAL SCIENCES ACTIVITIES
These activities connect the subject matter in the Student Edition with economics, civics, and science, technology, and society.

READING AND LANGUAGE ARTS
Some activities can facilitate the development of nonfiction reading strategies. Others help students' appreciation of fiction and poetry, focusing on word choice, description, and figurative language.

TEACHING GUIDE: CHAPTER SIDEBARS

Icons quickly help identify key concepts, facts, activities, and assessment activities in the sidebars.

▶ Cast of Characters
This sidebar points out and identifies significant personalities in the chapter. Pronunciation guides are included where necessary.

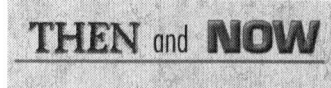

▶ Then and Now
This feature provides interesting facts and ideas about the ancient civilization and relates it to the modern world. This may be an aspect of government still in use today, word origins of common modern expressions, physical reminders of the past, and other features. You can use this item simply to promote interest in the subject matter or as a springboard to other research.

▶ Linking Disciplines
This feature offers opportunities to investigate other subject areas that relate to the material in the Student Edition: math, science, arts, and health. Specific areas of these subjects are emphasized: **Math** (arithmetic, algebra, geometry, data, statistics); **Science** (life science, earth science, physical science); **Arts** (music, arts, dance, drama, architecture); **Health** (personal health, world health).

▶ For Homework
A quick glance links you to additional activities in the Student Study Guide that can be assigned as homework.

ASSESSMENT

The Medieval & Early Modern World program intentionally omits from the Student Edition the kinds of section, chapter, and unit questions that are used to review and assess learning in standard textbooks. It is the purpose of the series to engage readers in learning—and loving—history written as good literature. Rather than interrupting student reading and enjoyment, all assessment instruments for the series have been placed in the Teaching Guides.

> ▶ **CHAPTER TESTS**
> A reproducible chapter test follows each chapter in this Teaching Guide. These tests will help you assess students' mastery of the content addressed in each chapter. These tests measure a variety of cognitive and analytical skills, particularly comprehension, critical thinking, and expository writing through multiple choice, short answer, and essay questions.
> *An answer key for the chapter tests is provided at the end of the Teaching Guide.*
>
> ▶ **WRAP-UP TEST**
> After the last chapter test you will find a wrap-up test consisting of 10 essay questions that evaluate students' ability to synthesize and express what they've learned about the civilization under study. Depending upon your class, you may want to consider assigning the questions as a takehome or open-book test.
>
> ▶ **RUBRICS**
> The rubrics at the back of this Teaching Guide will help you assess students' written work, oral presentations, and group projects. They include a Scoring Rubric based on standards for good writing and effective cooperative learning. In addition, a simplified hand-out is provided, plus a form for evaluating group projects and a Library/Media Center Research Log to help students focus and evaluate their research. Students can also evaluate their own work using these rubrics.
>
> ▶ **BLACKLINE MASTERS (BLMs)**
> Two blackline masters follow each chapter in the Teaching Guide. These BLMs are reproducible pages for you to use as in-class activities or homework exercises. Assigning primary source blackline masters to groups or partners is strongly encouraged, as this material may be quite challenging to some students. They can also be used for assessment as needed.
>
> ▶ **ADDITIONAL ASSESSMENT ACTIVITIES**
> The Group Project sections and Chapter Lessons of this Teaching Guide provide numerous activities and projects that have been designated as additional assessment opportunities, using the rubrics at the back of this Guide.

USING THE STUDENT STUDY GUIDE FOR ASSESSMENT

▶ Study Guide Activities
Assignments in the Student Study Guide correspond with those in the Teaching Guide. If needed, these Student Study Guide activities can be used for assessment.

▶ Portfolio Approach
Student Study Guide pages can be removed from the workbook and turned in for grading. When the pages are returned, they can be part of the students' individual history journals. Have students keep a 3-ring binder portfolio of Study Guide pages alongside writing projects and other activities.

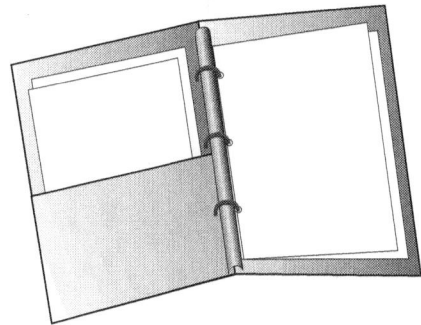

STUDENT STUDY GUIDE: KEY FEATURES

The Student Study Guide works as both standalone instructional material and as a support to the Student Edition and this Teaching Guide. Certain activities encourage informal small-group or family participation. These features make it an effective teaching tool:

Flexibility

You can use the Study Guide in the classroom, with individuals or small groups, or send it home for homework. You can distribute the entire guide to students; however, the pages are perforated so you can remove and distribute only the pertinent lessons.

A page on reports and special projects directs students to the "Further Reading" resource in the student edition. This feature gives students general guidance on doing research and devising independent study projects of their own.

> **FACSIMILE SPREAD**
> The Study Guide begins with a facsimile spread from the Student Edition. This spread gives reading strategies and highlights key features: captions, primary sources, sidebars, headings, etymologies. The spread supplies the contextualization students need to fully understand the material.

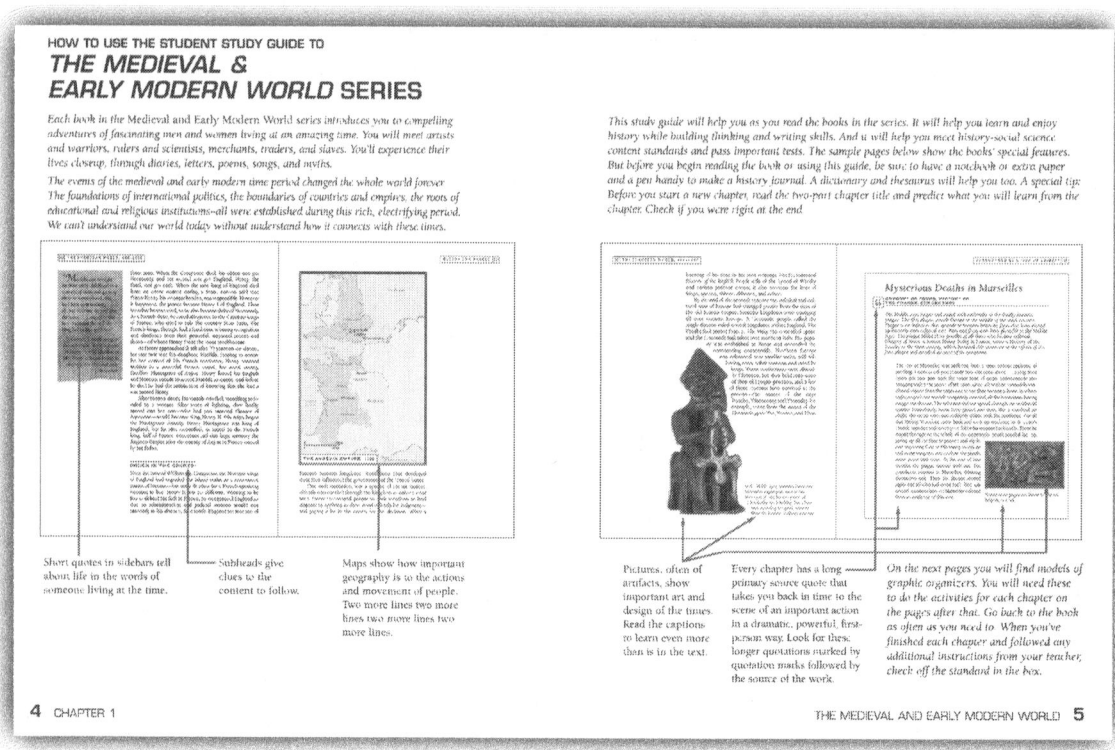

Portfolio Approach

The Study Guide pages are three-hole-punched so they can be integrated with notebook paper in a looseleaf binder. This history journal or portfolio can become both a record of content mastery and an outlet for each student's unique creative expression. Responding to prompts, students can write poetry or songs, plays and character sketches, create storyboards or cartoons, or construct multi-layered timelines.

The portfolio approach gives students unlimited opportunities for practice in areas that need strengthening. Students can share their journals and compare their work. And the Study Guide pages in the portfolio make a valuable assessment tool for you. The portfolio is an ongoing record of performance that can be reviewed and graded periodically.

GRAPHIC ORGANIZERS

This feature contains reduced models of seven graphic organizers referenced frequently in the study guide. Using these devices will help students organize the material so it is meaningful to them. (Full-size reproducibles of each graphic organizer are provided at the back of this Teaching Guide.) These graphic organizers include: outline, main idea map, K-W-L chart (What I Know, What I Want to Know, What I Learned), Venn diagram, timeline, sequence of events chart, and T-chart.

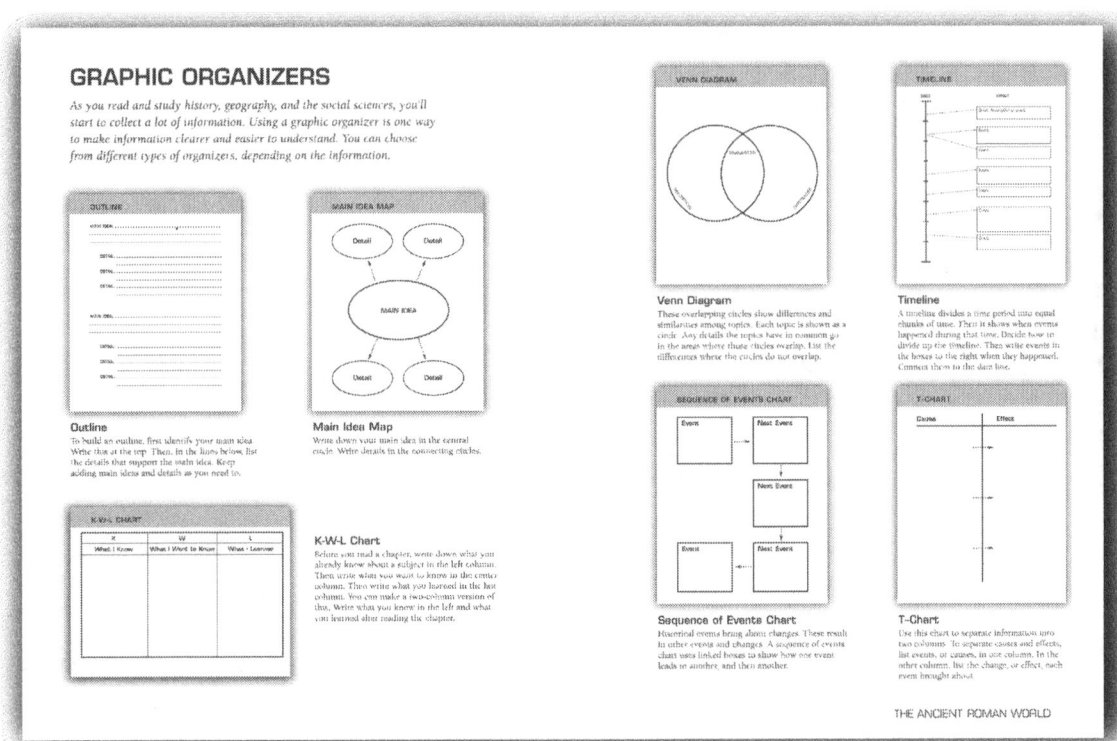

STUDENT STUDY GUIDE: CHAPTER LESSONS

Each chapter lesson is designed to draw students into the subject matter. Recurring features and exercises challenge their knowledge and allow them to practice valuable analysis and English language arts skills. Activities in the Teaching Guide and Student Study Guide complement but do not duplicate each other. Together they offer a wide range of class work, group projects, and opportunities for further study and assessment that can be tailored to all ability levels.

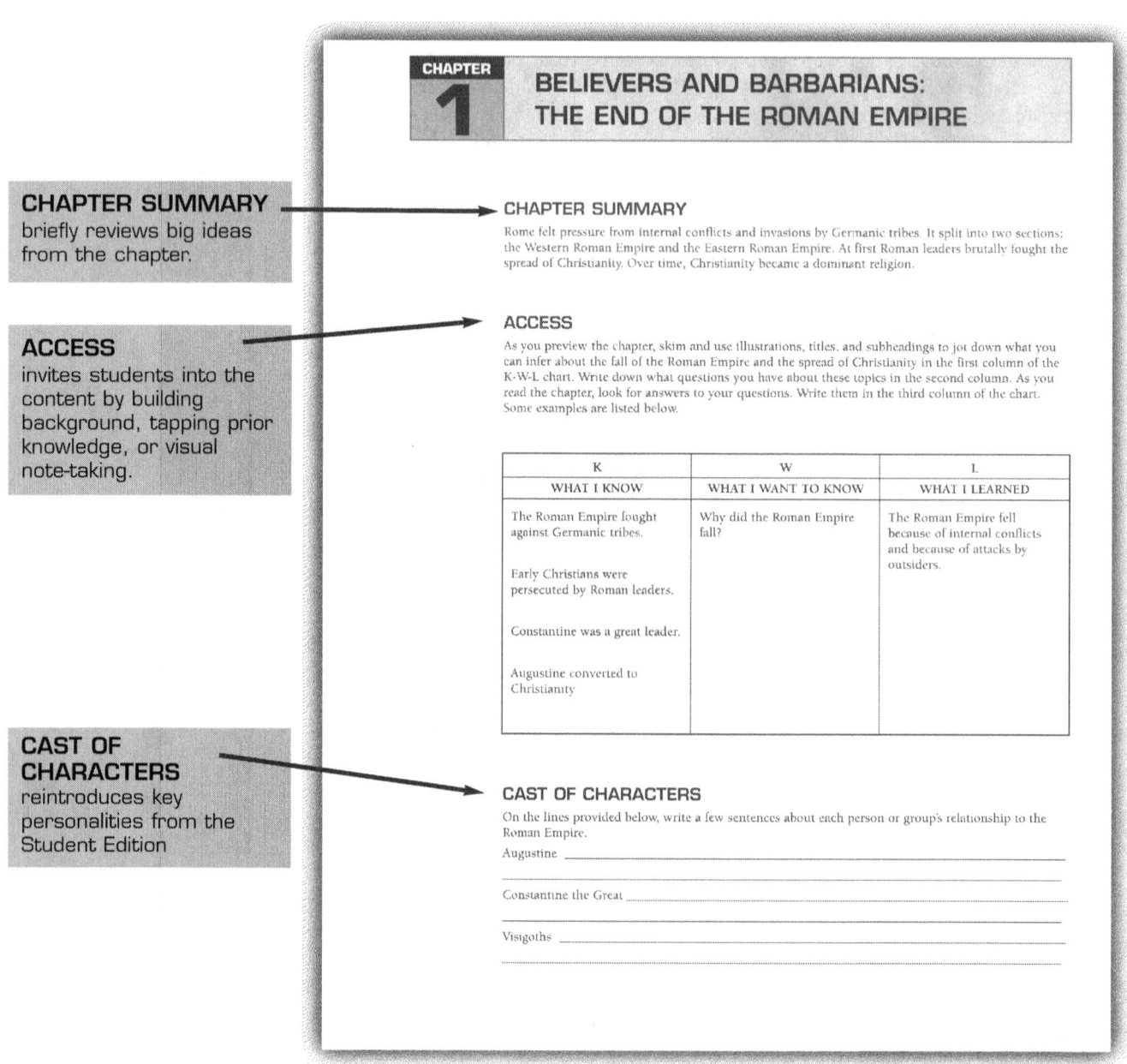

CHAPTER SUMMARY briefly reviews big ideas from the chapter.

ACCESS invites students into the content by building background, tapping prior knowledge, or visual note-taking.

CAST OF CHARACTERS reintroduces key personalities from the Student Edition

WORD BANK
reintroduces key curricular terms and difficult words from the Student Edition.

CRITICAL THINKING
exercises draw on such thinking skills as establishing cause and effect, making inferences, comparing and contrasting, identifying main ideas and details, and other analytical process.

WORKING WITH PRIMARY SOURCES
invites students to read primary sources closely. Exercises include DBQ's, evaluating point of view, and writing.

WRITE ABOUT IT
A writing assignment may stem from a vocabulary word, a historical event, or a primary source. The assignment can be a newspaper article, letter, short essay, a scene with dialogue, a diary entry.

ALL OVER THE MAP
uses engaging map skills activities to help students understand geography's crucial role in shaping history.

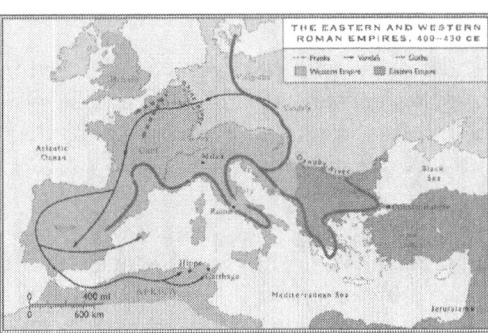

15

IMPROVING LITERACY WITH THE MEDIEVAL & EARLY MODERN WORLD

The books in this series are written in a lively, narrative style to inspire a love of reading history. English language learners and struggling readers are given special consideration within the program's exercises and activities. And students who love to read and learn will also benefit from the program's rich and varied material. Following are strategies to make sure each and every student gets the most out of the subjects you will teach through *The Medieval & Early Modern World*.

ENGLISH LANGUAGE LEARNERS

For English learners to achieve academic success, the instructional considerations for teachers include two mandates:

- Help them attain grade level, content area knowledge, and academic language.
- Provide for the development of English language proficiency.

To accomplish these goals, you should plan lessons that reflect the student's level of English proficiency. Students progress through five developmental levels as they increase in language proficiency:

Beginning and Early Intermediate (*grade level material will be mostly incomprehensible, students need a great deal of teacher support*)

Intermediate (*grade level work will be a challenge*)

Early Advanced and Advanced (*close to grade level reading and writing, students continue to need support*)

Refer to your state's ELD Standards for information about language proficiency at each level. The books in this program are written at the intermediate level. However, you can still use the lesson plans for students of different levels by using the strategies below:

Tap Prior Knowledge
What students know about the topic will help determine your next steps for instruction. Using K-W-L charts, brainstorming, and making lists are ways to find out what they know. English learners bring a rich cultural diversity into the classroom. By sharing what they know, students can connect their knowledge and experiences to the course.

Set the Context
Use different tools to make new information understandable. These can be images, artifacts, maps, timelines, illustrations, charts, videos, or graphic organizers. Techniques such as role-playing and story-boarding can also be helpful. Speak in shorter sentences, with careful enunciation, expanded explanations, repetitions, and paraphrasing. Use fewer idiomatic expressions.

Show—Don't Just Tell
English learners often get lost as they listen to directions, explanations, lectures, and discussions. By showing students what is expected, you can help them participate more fully in classroom activities. Students need to be shown how to use the graphic organizers in this guide and the mini versions in the student study guide, as well as other blackline masters for note-taking and practice. An overhead transparency with whole or small groups is also effective.

Use the Text
Because of unfamiliar words, students will need help. Teach them to preview the chapter using text features (headings, bold print, sidebars, italics). See the suggestions in the facsimile of the Student Edition, shown on pages 6–7 of the Student Study Guide. Show students organizing structures such as cause and effect or comparing and contrasting. Have students read to each other in pairs. Encourage them to share their history journals with each other. Use Read Aloud/Think Aloud, perhaps with an overhead transparency. Help them create word banks, charts, and graphic organizers. Discuss the main idea after reading.

Check for Understanding
Rather than simply ask students if they understand, stop frequently and ask them to paraphrase or expand on what you just said. Such techniques will give you a much clearer assessment of their understanding.

Provide for Interaction
As students interact with the information and speak their thoughts, their content knowledge and academic language skills improve. Increase interaction in the classroom through cooperative learning, small group work, and partner share. By working and talking with others, students can practice asking and answering questions.

Use Appropriate Assessment
When modifying the instruction, you will also need to modify the assessment. Multiple choice, true and false, and other criterion reference tests are suitable, but consider changing test format and structure. English learners are constantly improving their language proficiency in their oral and written responses, but they are often grammatically incorrect. Remember to be thoughtful and fair about giving students credit for their content knowledge and use of academic language, even if their English isn't perfect.

STRUGGLING READERS

Some students struggle to understand the information presented in a textbook. The following strategies for content-area reading can help students improve their ability to make comparisons, sequence events, determine importance, summarize, evaluate, synthesize, analyze, and solve problems.

Build Knowledge of Genre
Both the fiction and narrative nonfiction genres are incorporated into *The Medieval & Early Modern World*. This combination of genres makes the text interesting and engaging. But teachers must be sure students can identify and use the organizational structures of both genres.

Fiction	Nonfiction
Each chapter is a story	Content: historical information
Setting: historical time and place	Organizational structure: cause/effect, sequence of events, problem/solution
Characters: historical figures	Other features: maps, timelines, sidebars, photographs, primary sources
Plot: problems, roadblocks, and resolutions	

In addition, the textbook has a wealth of the text features of nonfiction: bold and italic print, sidebars, headings and subheadings, labels, captions, and "signal words" such as *first*, *next*, and *finally*. Teaching these organizational structures and text features is essential for struggling readers.

Build Background

Having background information about a topic makes reading about it so much easier. When students lack background information, teachers can preteach or "front load" concepts and vocabulary, using a variety of instructional techniques. Conduct a chapter or book walk, looking at titles, headings, and other text features to develop a big picture of the content. Focus on new vocabulary words during the "walk" and create a word bank with illustrations for future reference. Read aloud key passages and discuss the meaning. Focus on the timeline and maps to help students develop a sense of time and place. Show a video, go to a website, and have trade books and magazines on the topic available for student exploration.

Comprehension Strategies

While reading, successful readers are predicting, making connections, monitoring, visualizing, questioning, inferring, and summarizing. Struggling readers have a harder time with these "in the head" processes. The following strategies will help these students construct meaning from the text until they are able to do it on their own.

PREDICT: Before reading, conduct a picture and text feature "tour" of the chapter to make predictions. Ask students if they remember if this has ever happened before, to predict what might happen this time.

MAKE CONNECTIONS: Help students relate content to their background (text to text, text to self, and text to the world).

MONITOR AND CONFIRM: Encourage students to stop reading when they come across an unknown word, phrase, or concept. In their notebooks, have them make a note of text they don't understand and ask for clarification or figure it out. While this activity slows down reading at first, it is effective in improving skills over time.

VISUALIZE: Students benefit from imagining the events described in a story. Sketching scenes, story-boarding, role-playing, and looking for sensory details all help students with this strategy.

INFER: Help students look beyond the literal meaning of a text to understand deeper meanings. Graphic organizers and discussions provide opportunities to broaden their understanding. Looking closely at the "why" of historical events helps students infer.

QUESTION AND DISCUSS: Have students jot down their questions as they read, and then share them during discussions. Or have students come up with the type of questions they think a teacher would ask. Over time students will develop more complex inferential questions, which lead to group discussions. Questioning and discussing also helps students see ideas from multiple perspectives and draw conclusions, both critical skills for understanding history.

DETERMINE IMPORTANCE: Teach students how to decide what is most important from all the facts and details in nonfiction. After reading for an overall understanding, they can go back to highlight important ideas, words, and phrases. Clues for determining importance include bold or italic print, signal words, and other text features. A graphic organizer such as a main idea map also helps.

Teach and Practice Decoding Strategies

Rather than simply defining an unfamiliar word, teach struggling readers decoding strategies:

- Have them look at the prefix, suffix, and root to help figure out the new word.
- Look for words they know within the word.
- Use the context for clues, and read further or reread.

ADVANCED LEARNERS

Every classroom has students who finish the required assignments and then want additional challenges. Fortunately, the very nature of history and social science offers a wide range of opportunities for students to explore topics in greater depth. Encourage them to come up with their own ideas for an additional assignment. Determine the final product, its presentation, and a timeline for completion.

▶ Research

Students can develop in-depth understanding through seeking information, exploring ideas, asking and answering questions, making judgments, considering points of view, and evaluating actions and events. They will need access to a wide range of resource materials: the Internet, maps, encyclopedias, trade books, magazines, dictionaries, artifacts, newspapers, museum catalogues, brochures, and the library. See the "Further Reading" section at the end of the Student Edition for good jumping-off points.

▶ Projects

You can encourage students to capitalize on their strengths as learners (visual, verbal, kinesthetic, or musical) or to try a new way of responding. Students can prepare a debate or write a persuasive paper, play, skit, poem, song, dance, game, puzzle, or biography. They can create an alphabet book on the topic, film a video, do a book talk, or illustrate a book. They can render charts, graphs, or other visual representations. Allow for creativity and support students' thinking.

Cheryl A. Caldera, M.A.
Literacy Coach

GROUP PROJECTS

These interactive, multimedia projects give every student the chance to experience some aspect of life in *The Age of Science and Revolutions, 1600–1800* . They will add fun and depth to your exploration of this amazing time in history and can be used for assessment with the rubrics at the back of this Teaching Guide.

Chapter 1
▶ **Sail Away**

Explain to the class that the year is 1620, the place is England, and their task is to provision a 30-ton ship heading for North America carrying 10 sailors and 25 passengers. Ask: What kinds of essential supplies and equipment must the ship carry? What assumptions must you make to help you plan? Summarize students' suggestions on the board. Then divide students into groups of four to six to name their ship and create a list of provisions for it. Let students begin the project by brainstorming and skimming Chapter 1 for information and ideas. As homework, have students use the Internet and print resources to search for such primary resources as journals, memoirs, and ship's logs of the era as well as secondary sources to find out more about sea voyages during this period. After they complete their research, have the groups compile their list, discuss it, and revise it to reflect everyone's best ideas. For an authentic look, completed drafts can be published by choosing an "old-fashioned" or period computer font in a word-processing program and using it to input the copy. Finally, post provision lists in the classroom so that students can compare their list to the others. Share with the class the assessment rubric at the back of this guide.

Chapter 2
▶ **Objects Tell the Tale**

Ask pairs of students to work together on this project. Direct pairs to review the chapter with these questions in mind: What item would you choose to sum up one of the important points in the chapter? How could you represent it? For example, students might select a spice and display a small amount of it or a precious metal and make a "gold doubloon" to exemplify the age of mercantilism. They might choose manufactured goods such as cloth, shoes, or nails to discuss the ideas of Adam Smith or describe manufacturing processes. After pairs choose their object, they can do more research about it at home and make, collect, or illustrate their representation of it. Students should write a few bits of information about their item and its significance on an index card. Display the items and labels on a table in the classroom and have one student from each pair be on hand to answer questions as the rest of the class and perhaps a few invited visitors examine the objects and ask questions about them. Share with the class the assessment rubric at the back of this guide.

Chapter 3
▶ Grand Conversations

Explain to students that in this project they will have a chance to be someone else—at least for a little while. Have them choose an interesting person they read about in Chapter 3 such as Lufti Pasha, Suleiman the Magnificent, or Lady Mary Wortley Montagu. Urge students to reread the parts of the chapter that mentioned that person, and jot down a few notes about him or her. As homework, encourage students to do research to find out more about the person. Have them assemble a simple costume from such common household items as hats, scarves, gloves, cardboard, and aluminum foil. On the day selected for the grand conversation, students spend an hour or two being their chosen person: reacting to classroom happenings as that person, answering questions, and chatting with the other characters. Videotape or audiotape the grand conversations if possible so that parents and other students can enjoy them. Share with the class the assessment rubric at the back of this guide.

Chapter 4
▶ Daily News Flash

Have students work together in committees to produce a newspaper that reports events on a day during the reign of the Mughal Dynasty in India. To get started, let students choose among such committees as planning, research, writing, editing and proofreading, illustration, design, and inputting. Discuss with the class the duties of each committee and have the entire group brainstorm a title, format, and features for the newspaper. Emphasize that though the newspaper should be based on facts, articles can be as wild and wacky as students care to make them. Brainstorm some events that might be worth reporting such as the unveiling of the Peacock Throne, Akbar's expedition to Agra to rein in his wayward son, or Aurangzeb taking his father prisoner in the Great Red Fort. Students can work in committees during class time and continue research, writing, and other tasks as homework. Those with desktop publishing skills can use a computer to input final copy and art. Be sure to make enough copies of the newspaper for the school population and distribution to students' families. Share with the class the assessment rubric at the back of this guide.

Chapter 5
▶ **Who Was Who**

Ask students to write a biographical entry for Matteo Ricci or another person they read about in Chapter 5. Display a copy of *Marquis Who's Who* or a similar reference or print out a page from an online resource such as *www.marquiswhoswho.com*. Discuss the information a typical entry includes such as name, occupation, birth date, family, career highlights, achievements, and so on, but point out that students may not be able to find out information for all these categories and may want to add others. After students reread the information in the chapter about the subject of their biographical entry, have them write a draft and do further research at home. Compile completed biographies in a class Who Was Who volume, which students can donate to the class or school library. Share with the class the assessment rubric at the back of this guide.

Chapter 6
▶ **The Heart of the Matter**

Let small groups of students reenact Galileo's appearance before the Inquisition, when the great scientist was forced to renounce his belief in the Copernican system, in which the Earth and other planets revolve around the sun. Encourage students to do further research in class and as homework to find out as much as they can about what transpired during Galileo's ordeal, particularly what he and the Inquisitors said to each other. The person in each group who plays Galileo should write, and if possible memorize, a persuasive speech in support of Galileo's ideas. The rest of the group plays Inquisitors and improvises responses to the speech. Perhaps in one of these presentations Galileo can persuade the Inquisitors that his views are correct and do not contradict the Bible! Share with the class the assessment rubric at the back of this guide. As each group performs before the class, the rest of the students may want to rate its performance against the rubric.

Chapter 7
▶ How Cool Is That!

Ask students to choose an idea, invention, or discovery they learned about in the chapter that they found intriguing or about which they would like to learn more. They might choose, for example, the telescope, microscope, how blood flows in the body, or *Cogito, ergo sum*. After research time in class and as homework, have students take on the persona of a scientist or philosopher and present their chosen idea, invention, or discovery to the class. Let them bring from home simple costumes to wear if they like. Challenge students to explain the ideas in the clearest way they can, using props, diagrams, or illustrations whenever possible. Presenters should encourage questions from the audience. Share with the class the assessment rubric at the back of this guide. As each student presents before the class, the rest of the other students may want to rate his or her presentation against the rubric.

Chapter 8
▶ Book Jackets

Divide the class into pairs to create a book jacket for a work by Voltaire or for one of the titles discussed in Chapter 8 such as *Persian Letters* or Diderot's *Encyclopédie*. Discuss the parts (spine, front and back cover, flaps) and function of book jackets (to protect the book and attract buyers). After students choose a book, ask them to reread the information about it in their textbook and brainstorm ways to present the important ideas succinctly and enticingly. Encourage them to study as many book jackets as they can to learn what makes some jackets more appealing than others. As homework, have students find the book, read the table of contents, skim the text, and jot down points to include on the jacket. After working cooperatively to write the copy and produce cover art, ask volunteers to arrange an attractive display of book covers for the class to enjoy. If you like, have each pair introduce its book cover and explain some of the decisions that went into producing it. Share with the class the assessment rubric at the back of this guide.

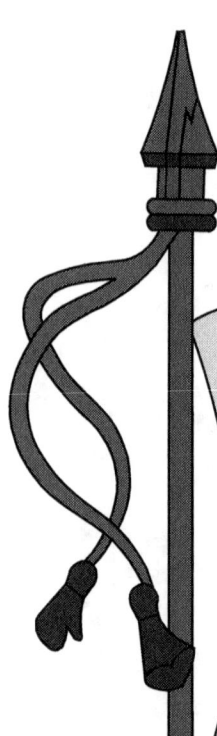

Chapter 9
▶ Obituary

Ask students to imagine that they have been assigned the sad responsibility of writing a short obituary of Caroline Herschel or one of the other women of the Enlightenment discussed in Chapter 9. After they choose a subject, their challenge is to sum up the woman's accomplishments and significance briefly but colorfully and passionately. As an extra challenge, ask them to think of a phrase or sentence to carve into the woman's headstone. Explain that the more they know about the woman, the easier their task will be, so ask students to do additional research about her as homework. Publish completed obituaries as a class book and let students vote on their favorite memorial inscription. Share with the class the assessment rubric at the back of this guide.

Chapter 10
▶ Tableaux Vivants

Divide the class into small groups. Ask each group to select an event they read about in Chapter 10 that they would like to depict in a tableau vivant, a scene with props and motionless and silent costumed actors. Urge students to choose dramatic events such as Grotius being smuggled out of jail in his book chest or the beheading of Charles I. Have groups brainstorm ideas and divvy up tasks involving props and costumes. Let students build simple props and assemble costumes at home. On performance day, station the tableaux vivants around the classroom and remind students to stay as still as they possibly can. Invite in another class to enjoy the tableaux vivants. After the performance is over, let students decompress by discussing the effectiveness of tableaux vivants and what it feels like to perform one. Share with the class the assessment rubric at the back of this guide. You may wish to have the audience rate the performances against the rubric.

CHAPTER LESSONS

- Teaching Strategies
- Blackline Masters
- Tests

CHAPTER 1

SETTLEMENTS, TRADE, AND CONFLICT: THE NORTH AMERICAN EXPERIENCE PAGES 19–33

FOR HOMEWORK

STUDENT STUDY GUIDE
pages 11–14

CHAPTER SUMMARY

During the 1600s, the English (who came to dominate Eastern North America by the mid-1700s) and other Europeans established precarious settlements in the region. The settlers' survival depended on aid from their Native American trading partners, vast numbers of whom died from European diseases to which they lacked immunity. As the Native American work force dwindled, the growing colonies began importing slaves from Africa.

PERFORMANCE OBJECTIVES

- ▶ To analyze the risks and rewards of European exploration and settlement of North America
- ▶ To understand how England came to dominate the region
- ▶ To compare and contrast the interactions of Europeans, Native Americans, and Africans in North America
- ▶ To explain the causes and effects of slavery

BUILDING BACKGROUND

Challenge students to exercise their imaginations by traveling back in time. Have them imagine they are English settlers of the 1600s seeing the coast of Maine for the first time; Native Americans observing the settlers' arrival; and African slaves, who, having survived the middle passage, are on the auction block. If these people could speak freely and understand each other, what would they say? Encourage students to reconsider their ideas about these groups as they read the chapter.

VOCABULARY

peninsula land that is surrounded by water on three sides

alliance a close association or agreement

dominion control

monopoly exclusive control over a commercial activity

As needed, have students consult the glossary to define the following words: *malaria, sassafras, shallop*.

CAST OF CHARACTERS

Bartholomew Gosnold English sea captain who discovered the coast of what is now Maine

Olaudah (oh-LAU-dah) **Equiano** (eh-kwee-AHN-o) African slave who bought his freedom, wrote his autobiography, and became a prominent English abolitionist

WORKING WITH PRIMARY SOURCES

Have students speculate about Olaudah Equiano's character and his influence. What kind of man would buy his freedom after a decade of slavery and go on to write one of the first works in English by a former slave? Tell students that *The Interesting Narrative* was a best seller in its time, as popular as *Robinson Crusoe* and published in many editions and languages. Note that Equiano played a major part in the abolitionist movement in England (http://atomicage.com/equiano/life.html; http://pbs.org/wghb/aia/part1/1p276.html).

READING COMPREHENSION QUESTIONS

1. What were some of the ways Captain Gosnold and his passengers tried to profit from their voyages to North America? *(by collecting sassafras and cedar)*
2. What were good and bad characteristics of the location the colonists on the *Godspeed* chose for their new settlement, Jamestown? *(good: deep water allowed ships to load and unload easily; bad: swampy, mosquito-infested land; high tide covered much of the land; the land was in Indian territory)*
3. What was Powhatan's message to the Englishmen? Did it make good sense? *(He urged peaceful cooperation. Most students will believe his message made sense because the settlers could not survive without the Indians' help, and the Native Americans wanted to live peaceful lives.)*
4. Why did the colonists turn to Africa for slaves when they faced a labor shortage? *(Africans had been traded as slaves in Africa, the Middle East, and Europe for centuries, and Europeans were used to traveling to Africa for slaves.)*

CRITICAL THINKING QUESTIONS

1. The first European settlers in North America faced incredible hardships, and many of them did not survive their first winter. Yet, colonists continued to travel to North America. Why? *(Despite the hardships, the New World held the promise of prosperity and religious freedom that was lacking in Europe.)*
2. Which group benefited more from the lively trade that took place between them, the Native Americans or the Europeans? Why? *(Possible answer: The Europeans benefited more because they traded for the food they needed to avoid starvation. The Indians got useful but not essential items, such as tools and weapons of iron and steel.)*
3. Why do you think Olaudah Equiano wrote his autobiography? *(Possible answer: to describe the horrors of slavery so that people would abolish the practice.)*

SOCIAL SCIENCES

Science, Technology, and Society Certain European technologies and inventions enabled the Europeans to explore the world, trade successfully, and subdue native peoples. Have small groups of students choose a European technology or invention that the Native Americans lacked, research it, and explain how the Europeans used it to their advantage.

READING AND LANGUAGE ARTS

Reading Nonfiction Remind students that because every historical event happens for a reason and every one has an effect, identifying causes and effects will help them understand historical accounts. The effects of European settlement of North America, such as the use of Africans as slaves can be felt to this day. Have students chart the causes of African slavery and its immediate and long-term effects.

Using Language In part because he wrote his autobiography, the true story of his life, people today know who Olaudah Equiano was and what his life was like. Ask students to write about an incident in their life they would like people in the future to remember.

THEN and NOW

Slavery exists in the world today only as a memory, correct? Wrong! Though the 1927 Slavery Convention declared the practice illegal worldwide, millions of people in every part of the world are enslaved today. (http://iabolish.com).

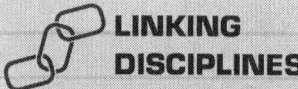

LINKING DISCIPLINES

Math Have students research a 17th-century sailing voyage from a European port to a site in North America. Ask students to figure out the approximate distance of the trip and how long it lasted. Then have them calculate how many miles per day the ship traveled. Let students compare that figure to the speed of an airplane following the same route.

WRITING

Interview Ask students which one of the people they read about in the chapter they would like to meet most. What would they ask that person about his life, beliefs, and hopes for the future? Ask students to write a mock interview with the person they chose. Encourage students who wrote about the same people to compare interviews.

SUPPORTING LEARNING

English Language Learners Help students label an illustration that features an old-time sailing ship with words in the chapter related to sailing and the sea. These include *hull*, *deck*, *sails*, *crew*, *crow's nest*, and *shoal*, among others. Encourage students to add new labels to the illustration as they encounter them in the text and to use the illustration to jog their memories of the words' meanings.

Struggling Readers As students read the chapter, have them write a one-sentence summary for each person mentioned in the text. Each sentence should explain who the person was and what the person did. Encourage students to reread the sentences to review what they learned in the chapter.

EXTENDING LEARNING

Enrichment Have students read *The Interesting Narrative of the Life of Olaudah* and choose a vivid passage to read aloud to the class. Then have them lead a class discussion about the influence of Equiano's autobiography and other slave narratives on the abolitionist movement.

Extension Let pairs of students take the parts of Captain John Smith and Powhatan and role-play a meeting between the two leaders. Then have students switch parts and reenact the meeting. Encourage students to discuss how their words and feelings changed depending on which part they played.

LITERATURE CONNECTION

The following books of historical fiction will broaden students' knowledge about life in the North American settlements. You may want to advise students that historical fiction is not always accurate in details.

Hermes, Patricia. *Our Strange New Land: Elizabeth's Jamestown Colony Diary*. New York: Scholastic, 2000. Describes how in May 1607, three British ships sailed up the James River in Virginia, carrying men who established the first permanent English colony in Jamestown, Virginia. In 1609, after 71 days at sea, the first ship carrying women and children arrived, including 9-year-old Elizabeth Baker.

Ruemmler, John. *Smoke on the Water: A Novel of Jamestown and the Powhatans*. New York: Shoe Tree Press, 1992. Near Jamestown in 1622, a young English boy and the son of a Powhatan Indian chief find themselves caught up in the growing animosity between their peoples.

Rockwood, Joyce. *To Spoil the Sun*. New York: Holt, 2003. Omens forewarn Rain Dove and the other Cherokee Indians who live in a 16th-century village in the southern Appalachians of the disease and upheaval to come following the arrival of Spanish explorers. After smallpox strikes, life for the people of the Seven Clans will never be the same.

LITERACY TIPS

In addition to using the suggestions in the Supporting Learning and Extending Learning sections, refer back frequently to pages 16–19 for strategies and advice from a literacy coach.

NAME   **DATE**

AN AGE OF SCIENCE & REVOLUTIONS, 1600–1800

Directions

Study the map at the left.
Then answer the questions.

1. Which two explorers traveled inland?

_____
_____
_____
_____
_____
_____

2. By looking at the map, how is it likely that they traveled?

_____
_____
_____
_____
_____
_____
_____
_____

EXPLORING AND SETTLING THE ATLANTIC COAST, 1602–1750

- Area of settlement by 1750
- ---▶ Bartholomew Gosnold, 1602
- ⇒ Henry Hudson, 1609
- ▶ John Smith, 1607–1608

3. According to the map, from where is it likely Gosnold and Hudson came?
_____
_____
_____

4. To where is it likely Gosnold returned?
_____
_____
_____

CHAPTER 1 BLM   AN AGE OF SCIENCE & REVOLUTIONS, 1600–1800

An Age of Science & Revolutions, 1600–1800

Directions

In the first quotation below, from Englishman William Strachey's *Historie of Travell*, published in 1612, the author describes his reaction to Powhatan, about whom you read in this chapter. In the second, New England colonist Thomas Morton describes some Indians in *New English Canaan*, 1637.

Read the quotes. Then respond to the prompts.

    a. "[S]uch Majestie . . . which oftentimes strykes awe and sufficient wonder in our people . . ."

    b. "[T]o give their character in a worde, they are as proper men and women for feature and limbes as can be founde, for flesh and bloud as active."

IN YOUR OWN WORDS

1. Paraphrase the two quotations. Use everyday contemporary English.

    a. _____

    b. _____

2. Based on Strachey's words and what you learned about the Native American leader in this chapter, how would you describe Powhatan?

3. Did Morton's description of the Indians surprise you in any way? Why or why not?

4. Compare the tone of the two quotations.

NAME _____ DATE _____

A. COMPREHENSION

Circle the letter of the best answer to each question.

1. Who preceded the English in establishing settlements in the New World?
   a. the French and Italians
   b. the Chinese and Japanese
   c. the Spanish and Portuguese
   d. the Dutch and Scandinavians

2. Which was **not** a reason that Englishmen such as Bartholomew Gosnold sailed to North America?
   a. to become fur traders
   b. to settle in colonies
   c. to bring back items to sell
   d. to discover a northwest passage

3. Why did the passengers on the *Godspeed* choose to settle in what became Jamestown?
   a. There were plenty of friendly Indians.
   b. The land was swampy.
   c. When the tide came in, it covered the area.
   d. Deep water let ships come in close.

4. What was Powhatan's message to Captain John Smith?
   a. Cooperate with us and live in peace.
   b. Obey us or we will conquer you.
   c. Leave our lands immediately.
   d. Hire us because we know the land.

5. Why were slaves brought to the New World?
   a. Africans were interested in working in a new country.
   b. Southern colonies were growing many crops and needed a workforce.
   c. Native Americans were refusing to work.
   d. They were unhappy in their African homeland.

6. What did Olaudah Equiano mean when he described the slaves by writing, "every one of their countenances expressing dejection"?
   a. The slaves' faces hinted at a possible rebellion.
   b. The slaves' faces expressed hope and anticipation.
   c. The slaves' faces showed how sad they felt.
   d. The slaves' faces revealed their exhaustion.

B. SHORT ANSWER

Answer each question in several complete sentences.

7. Why was Captain Bartholomew Gosnold important to the story of the settlement of North America?

8. From his conversation with John Smith, how would you describe Powhatan as a leader?

9. In what ways was Olaudah Equiano's life different from that of most Africans sold into slavery in the New World?

C. ESSAY

On a separate piece of paper, write a few paragraphs to summarize the events in the chapter. Be sure to include the important people and their contributions.

CHAPTER 2

RUDE AWAKENINGS: WEALTH REDEFINED
PAGES 34–45

FOR HOMEWORK

STUDENT STUDY GUIDE
pages 15–18

CAST OF CHARACTERS

Antonio De (ahn-TOH-nee-o duh) **Ulloa** (oo-LYO-uh) naval officer who was part of a French and Spanish scientific expedition sent to Peru in 1735.

Adam Smith father of modern economics and author of *The Wealth of Nations*

John Wesley English minister and the founder of Methodism

CHAPTER SUMMARY

During the age of mercantilism of the 17th and 18th centuries, England, Spain, France, and Holland battled for the wealth of the New World, which included precious metals and spices. Economic battles led to piracy and war. Adam Smith, the founder of modern economics, argued in *The Wealth of Nations* that free trade and competition could bring prosperity to all nations.

PERFORMANCE OBJECTIVES

▶ To define mercantilism and describe its effects on European countries and their colonies

▶ To compare and contrast the ideas about wealth held by various European countries

▶ To analyze arguments about true wealth set forth in Adam Smith's *The Wealth of Nations*

▶ To describe the reasons for innovations in English manufacturing and the decline in the Spanish economy

▶ To understand John Wesley's concerns about the effect of wealth on religion

BUILDING BACKGROUND

Ask students what the term "the law of supply and demand" means and whether this law is followed strictly in the United States today. After a brief discussion of the controls the U.S. and all governments place on unfettered capitalism, explain that the mercantilism of the 17th and 18th centuries was a free-for-all, with each European country that had a presence in the New World struggling for a monopoly on trade. Urge students to think about how well this system worked and what a nation's true wealth is as they read the chapter.

VOCABULARY

quotas production assignments

fleet warships under one command

invincible unconquerable

methodical arranged in a regular, systematic order

diligent marked by painstaking effort

frugal economical, sparing

exhort urge by arguments or appeals

As needed, have students consult the glossary to define the following words: *mercantilism, quota.*

WORKING WITH PRIMARY SOURCES

During this period spices such as cloves, nutmeg, and cinnamon were rare imports from far-off islands and great treasures to Europeans. Coffee, too, was an exotic new treat with its own culture and traditions. Read aloud the excerpt from Antoine Galland's *On the Origin and Development of Coffee* that appears on page 115 of *The Medieval & Early Modern World Primary Sources and Reference Volume*. Discuss students' reactions to the piece. If no one mentions it, point out how contemporary the coffee-related customs Galland describes seem.

GEOGRAPHY CONNECTION

Movement Have students look at the trade map on page 38 of their books. Ask students to describe the trade routes and to discuss the areas claimed by the various countries. Have them compare which countries had the most direct routes to the lands they claimed and which had to travel the most. Have students speculate as to why these countries would want to travel to these places and claim these areas for themselves.

READING COMPREHENSION QUESTIONS

1. Which aspect of the economic system of Peru distressed scientist Antonio De Ulloa? (*the near-slavery and harsh working conditions under which the natives labored*)
2. Why were spices just as valuable as precious metals? (*Spices were rare, expensive, and very profitable imports.*)
3. What were trading companies, and why were they founded? (*Trading companies were sponsored by the state along with groups of merchants. Their purpose was to band together to try to create monopolies on precious items such as spices.*)
4. According to Adam Smith in *The Wealth of Nations*, what is the "invisible hand" and what is its effect? (*The invisible hand is competition; its effect is to keep sellers honest.*)

CRITICAL THINKING QUESTIONS

1. Why did it turn out to be not quite true that the more gold and silver a country had, the richer it was? (*Stockpiling wealth caused inflation. Merchants were able to charge so much more for their goods that many formerly wealthy landowners could no longer pay. When they lost their land, the peasants working for them lost their livelihood, too.*)
2. Why might some people consider *The Wealth of Nations* as important a document as the Declaration of Independence? (*Possible answer:* The Wealth of Nations *gave readers a revolutionary new way of thinking about how economies work and why free trade benefits everyone.*)
3. Why did Smith believe that industriousness is the real basis of a country's wealth? (*Possible answer: because industriousness cannot be used up and new inventions and improvements that result from industriousness can continue to generate wealth.*)

SOCIAL SCIENCES

Economics Distribute the blackline master of quotations from *The Wealth of Nations*. Ask students to restate the quotations in their own words and give examples from their experience that illustrate the accuracy of Adam Smith's analysis.

THEN and NOW

The ideas of Adam Smith and his followers are today called classical economics. Every modern economist has read and been influenced by *The Wealth of Nations* no matter what the person's reaction to Smith's ideas.

AN AGE OF SCIENCE AND REVOLUTIONS, 1600–1800

LINKING DISCIPLINES

Science Students can research the various spices that traders imported from Indonesia's spice islands. Challenge students to find out what part of the plant each popular spice came from and how it was used. They can present their findings in informal talks and illustrations.

READING AND LANGUAGE ARTS

Reading Nonfiction Ask students to describe the author's point of view toward Adam Smith and Smith's *The Wealth of Nations*. Draw their attention to the author's description of Smith as "one particularly brilliant thinker" and *The Wealth of Nations* as "the book that made him [Smith] famous." Encourage students to identify other passages that reveal the author's opinion of Smith and his work.

Using Language Students may enjoy learning the etymology of the word *economy*. They can explain how that original meaning, which can be traced to the Greek word for someone who manages a household, relates to the social science of economics.

WRITING

Advertisement Suppose that modern media and advertising techniques existed in the 17th century. Write a magazine advertisement or the script for a television commercial for a new and amazing beverage: coffee. Be as persuasive as you can.

SUPPORTING LEARNING

English Language Learners Ask students to make a chart of the proper nouns in the chapter. Have them title the chart *Proper Nouns* and list three headings: *People, Places,* and *Things,* then write each proper noun they encounter in the chapter under the appropriate heading. Remind students that the names of particular people, places, and things are capitalized in English. When students have completed their charts, have volunteers read the words. Help them pronounce the proper nouns as necessary, and explain how each proper noun relates to the content of the chapter.

Struggling Readers Have students read aloud John Wesley's letter (Student Edition page 41) sentence by sentence. After each sentence is read, ask a volunteer to restate it in simpler, more contemporary language. Ask: What is Wesley saying here? How would someone express this thought today? Provide assistance as necessary. Then have students use the main idea map graphic organizer (see reproducibles at the back of this guide) to analyze Wesley's ideas.

EXTENDING LEARNING

Enrichment Ask volunteers to find out more about David Hume's *Treatise of Human Nature*, the book that landed Adam Smith in so much trouble at Oxford. Have students discuss why the book was considered dangerous and how Hume's ideas might have influenced Smith.

Extension Have small groups of students work together to choose one of the inventions of the 18th century, such as the steam engine, that impacted improvements in industry. Then ask students to do research on this invention and make posters showing how the invention works. Ask a representative or representatives from each group to present the posters to the class, explain them, and answer questions about the invention their group chose.

LITERACY TIPS

In addition to using the suggestions in the Supporting Learning and Extending Learning sections, refer back frequently to pages 16–19 for strategies and advice from a literacy coach.

NAME   **DATE**

Directions

Read the quotations from "The *Tiger* Journal of the 1585 Voyage," in *The Roanoke Voyages*, ed. David B. Quinn. Then answer the questions.

> About the 31 [August 1585] he [Sir Richard Grenville] tooke a Spanish ship of 300. Tunne richly loaden, boording her with a boate made with goards of chests, which fell a sunder, and sunke at the shippes side, as soon as ever hee and his men were out of it.
>
> . . . the squadron left Bideford . . . [and] soon began to encounter merchant ships coming from Spain. One, an English ship, the *Angel of Topsham*, was stopped and Grenville took some wine and oil. . . . a few days later . . . a number of other vessels were sighted, two of which Grenville boarded and took.

1. What is the author describing in these passages?

2. How would you characterize Sir Richard Grenville's activities? What would you call him?

3. From context, try to determine the meaning of these words: *Tunne, loaden, goards, a sunder*.

4. Would you like to have been a member of Sir Grenville's crew? Give reasons for your answer.

CHAPTER 2 BLM
AN AGE OF SCIENCE & REVOLUTIONS, 1600–1800

NAME　　　　　　　　　　　　　　　　　　DATE

Directions

Read the excerpt from John Wesley's letter to the leader of another congregation in 1786, in which he worries about the effect of wealth on religion. Then write whether each statement is true or false. If it is false, rewrite it so that it is true.

> I fear, wherever riches have increased, the essence of religion has decreased, in the same proportion. Therefore, I do not see how it is possible, in the nature of things, for any true revival of religion to continue long. For religion must necessarily produce both industry and frugality, and these cannot but produce riches. But as riches increase, so will pride, anger, and love of the world in all its branches. How then is it possible that Methodism, that is, a religion of the heart, though it flourishes now as a green bay tree, should continue in this state? For the Methodists in every place grow diligent and frugal; consequently they increase in goods. Hence they proportionately increase in pride, in anger, in the desire of the flesh, the desire of the eyes, and the pride of life. So, although the form of religion remains, the spirit is swiftly vanishing away. Is there no way to prevent this—this continual decay of pure religion? We ought not to prevent people from being diligent and frugal; we must exhort all Christians to gain all they can and to save all they can; that is, in effect to grow rich.

1. John Wesley believes that the richer people get, the more religious they become.

_____
_____
_____
_____

2. Wesley writes that religious people are frugal and industrious, so they can't help but gain wealth.

_____
_____
_____
_____

3. Wesley believes that "the pride of life" is a good quality for people to have.

_____
_____
_____
_____

4. Wesley presents the solution to the problem of maintaining "the essence of religion" at the end of his letter.

_____
_____
_____
_____

NAME _____ DATE _____

A. COMPREHENSION

Circle the letter of the best answer for each question.

1. What was the main reason spices such as cloves and cinnamon were so valuable to European traders?
   a. because consumers wanted them for their delicious taste
   b. because of their medicinal properties
   c. because they came from the spice islands
   d. because of their rarity traders could make a great deal of money

2. Which was **not** a goal of the trading companies?
   a. to establish colonies
   b. to encourage free trade
   c. to gain monopolies
   d. to start trading posts

3. Why did officials require Peruvian natives who worked in the mills to keep their hair long?
   a. so they could be readily distinguished from the Spaniards
   b. so their heads could stay warmer
   c. so their bosses could pull their hair if they did not behave
   d. so they could be tied to horses' tails and dragged to work

4. Another term for bounty hunting is
   a. treasure hunting.
   b. naval operations.
   c. piracy.
   d. war.

5. Why did the British, Dutch, French, and Spanish navies battle each other in the 17th and 18th centuries?
   a. to show the world which country was strongest
   b. to rule the other countries
   c. to win the greatest number of colonies and trading posts
   d. to gain control over natural resources

6. Why was Adam Smith forbidden to read David Hume's *Treatise of Human Nature* at Oxford?
   a. It argued against the Christian belief in miracles.
   b. It encouraged readers to stop going to church.
   c. It was too difficult for an undergraduate to understand.
   d. It made Christians seem like bad people.

B. SHORT ANSWER

Answer each question in several complete sentences.

7. According to Adam Smith, why did competition keep merchants from being too greedy?

_____
_____

8. How did the factory make manufacturing more efficient?

_____
_____

C. ESSAY

On a separate piece of paper write a few paragraphs explaining the meaning of mercantilism. Then discuss whether Adam Smith was a supporter of mercantilism and why you do or do not think so.

MOST MAGNIFICENT: THE OTTOMAN EMPIRE PAGES 46–59

STUDENT STUDY GUIDE
pages 19–22

CAST OF CHARACTERS

Kochu Bey (ko-CHOO BAY) Albanian or Macedonian scholar, entered royal service as Lufti Pasha had; became Grand Vizier in early 17th century

Lufti Pasha (loof-TEE pah-SHA) Albanian or Macedonian scholar, recruited as a young boy to serve in Ottoman Empire, who became Gran Vizier in mid-16th century; described his life in an autobiography

Albert Bobovi (Ali Bey) Polish page who lived and worked in the Sultan's palace in the 1630s and wrote an unauthorized report of what he saw

Suleiman I Ottoman ruler known as "The Magnificent" and "The Lawgiver"

Sinan (see-NAHN) renowned Ottoman architect who rebuilt Istanbul for Suleiman I

CHAPTER SUMMARY

One practice that kept the Ottoman Empire great was the collection system, in which young non-Muslim boys were taken from their families and educated. The brightest attended school at court and went into royal service. Outside the Sultan's palace, education focused on learning the Quran. In the early 1600s Kochu Bey wrote about the greatest of sultans, Suleiman the Magnificent, or "The Lawgiver." Not only was he just, he oversaw the building of mosques and palaces considered masterpieces of engineering and art. A rage for all things Turkish took hold in Europe.

PERFORMANCE OBJECTIVES

- To understand why the Ottoman Empire is called "magnificent"
- To describe both religious and secular education in the Ottoman Empire
- To analyze contributions to law, art, and architecture of Suleiman the Magnificent
- To understand Lady Mary Wortley Montagu's writing about the Ottoman Empire
- To analyze the effects of Ottoman culture on Europe and European culture and contacts on the Ottoman Empire

BUILDING BACKGROUND

Ask students to recall what they know about the Ottoman Empire and develop purposes for reading by filling out a K-W-L chart similar to the one found at the back of this guide. Students can work in groups to list some information they already know about the topic and generate study questions. Urge students to return to the chart after they finish reading the chapter to see whether all their questions were answered or whether they would like to do further research on these or other questions that occurred to them as they read the chapter.

VOCABULARY

converted adopted a new religion
elite superior group
just honorable and fair in his dealings
mosque Moslem house of worship
niche recess in a wall
bazaars markets of streets lined with stores and stalls

As needed, have students consult the glossary to define the following words: *devshirme, inoculation, mausoleum, mosque.*

WORKING WITH PRIMARY SOURCES

To help students understand the origin of the Ottoman Empire and the attitudes of the Ottoman Turk victors toward the Christians they defeated, have them read and discuss "Turkish Delight," on page 76 of the *The Medieval & Early Modern World Primary Sources and Reference Volume.* Read aloud the introduction and Sultan Muhammad's words as transcribed in this Serbian manuscript of 1510. Initiate a discussion about the passage. Ask: Do you think the Ottoman Turks were unique among victorious armies in attributing their victory to the will of God?

GEOGRAPHY CONNECTION

Regions Have students look at the map of the Ottoman Empire in 1683 on page 46 of the student book. Ask students to explain the shape of the empire an how it has spread. *(It takes its shape from the seas and seem to have spread around these areas of water.)* Elicit that the Ottoman Empire must have been very strong if it had control of this many waterways.

READING COMPREHENSION QUESTIONS

1. Why was Skanderbeg a hero in Albania 500 years ago? *(He defeated the Ottoman Turk soldiers who were trying to take his castle.)*

2. What was the collection and why did it occur? *(The collection was the taking of young Christian and other non-Muslim boys from their families throughout the Ottoman Empire. It was intended to keep the boys' families in line and to provide educated workers for the Empire.)*

3. What was typical education in the Ottoman Empire like? *(It was religious education in which a primary goal was to memorize the Quran.)*

4. What is the centerpiece of Muslim architecture and how is it adapted to its purpose? *(the mosque; it has a large open space for prayer, a tower for calling people to prayer, and a prayer niche to make sure worshippers face Mecca.)*

5. What were some Turkish imports that became popular in Europe? *(tulips, Turkish baths, coffee and coffeehouses, carpets, long-haired cats, marching bands, The Thousand and One Nights, croissants, turbans)*

CRITICAL THINKING QUESTIONS

1. Why was Lady Mary Wortley Montagu a remarkable woman for her time? *(She was adventuresome, kept an open mind about the Turks, and wrote influential travel books about her experiences in the Ottoman Empire.)*

2. The Ottomans were not particularly excited about European culture. Why do you think this was? *(Possible answer: They might have felt that their religious beliefs were threatened by the European scientific instruments and their employment practices by printing presses. Most people just did not like the way European food tasted. They also had an exciting culture of their own and an educated bureaucracy.)*

3. What evidence proves the importance of the Ottoman Empire? *(Possible answer: Their art, architecture, and literature remain admired today; the Ottoman Empire lasted longer than any other in the history of the world.)*

SOCIAL SCIENCES

Civics The Ottoman Empire was an autocracy that took boys from their families as tribute. Yet the collection system was admired by many Europeans. Why was this? Have students answer this question. Let them compare and contrast European forms of government of the 17th and 18th centuries with that of the Ottoman Empire.

THEN and NOW

Travelers still enjoy exploring faraway and exotic places just as Lady Mary Wortley Montagu did. But these days, there are very few places on earth that remain unexplored. For example, thousands of people a year attempt to climb Mt. Everest. More than 1,000 have made it to the top.

LINKING DISCIPLINES

Art Students can represent one of Sinan's beautiful mosques, bridges, aqueducts, or other structures in two or three dimensions. Let students choose the art medium they prefer.

READING AND LANGUAGE ARTS

Reading Nonfiction Ask students to look closely at the title of the chapter and of the headings, the captions, the map, words in italic type, and the other features in the chapter that are frequently found in nonfiction selections. Have students discuss how these features help them understand the text.

Using Language Draw students' attention to the word *devshirme*, which appears on the second page of the chapter. Note that the word is defined when it is introduced and point out that authors often define difficult or unusual words, especially ones in foreign languages. Challenge students to find other examples of words that are defined in the text (*katib, Muteferrika, vizierate, Hafiz, muezzin*).

WRITING

Journal Ask students to imagine that they have been taken from their family as a tribute to the sultan. Have them write a journal entry describing their first day in captivity.

SUPPORTING LEARNING

English Language Learners Point out to students that people long ago spelled some English words differently from the way they are spelled today. Review Lady Wortley Montagu's letter, substituting the contemporary spelling for each unconventional spelling. Offer a few examples to students such as *writ* (written) and *refflexion* (reflection) to help students get started.

Struggling Readers Have students use a sequence of events chart (see reproducibles at the back of this guide) to help them understand the collection system. Ask them to imagine that a boy was taken from his family as tribute. What happened to him? Have students use the chart to help them understand the sequence of events that typically took place.

EXTENDING LEARNING

Enrichment Students can find out more about the architecture of the Ottoman Empire. Have volunteers choose a favorite building, find out as much as they can about it, and gather illustrations of it. Then have them present the information they've found about the building to the class. Encourage them to display the illustrations, describe the building's special features, and answer their classmates' questions.

Extension Let a small group of student actors write a one-act play about *devshirme*, the collection, and perform it for the class. Encourage the group to provide information about the collection in their play as well as making it as exciting as they can.

LITERACY TIPS

In addition to using the suggestions in the Supporting Learning and Extending Learning sections, refer back frequently to pages 16-19 for strategies and advice from a literacy coach.

CHAPTER BLM 3
An Age of Science & Revolutions, 1600–1800

NAME   **DATE**

Directions

Read the two quotations. Then answer the questions.

> From the time that they first enter the school of the Grand Seraglio [palace] they are exceedingly well-directed. Day by day they are continuously instructed in good and comely behavior, in the discipline of the senses, in military prowess, and in a knowledge of the Moslem faith; in a word, in all the virtues of mind and body.
>
> Ottaviano Bon, *Il serreglio del gran signore* (1608)

> It should be understood, first of all, that the whole establishment of the sultan's court, the foundation of his empire, and the strength of his army, depend upon a permanent seminary of young boys.
>
> Blaise de Vigenere (1660)

1. What system that you read about in the chapter is described in these quotes?

_____
_____
_____
_____

2. You know that the boys did not enter the school of the Grand Seraglio willingly. Yet the second quote explains that the whole foundation of the empire rests on them. How do you think these boys become dependable in court and on the battlefield?

_____
_____
_____
_____

3. Overall, do you think the collection system was good for the boys who participated in it or bad for them? Explain.

_____
_____
_____
_____

CHAPTER 3 BLM
AN AGE OF SCIENCE & REVOLUTIONS, 1600–1800

Directions

Read the excerpt from the letter Lady Mary Wortley Montagu sent to Sarah Chiswell on April 1, 1717. Then answer the questions.

> I am going to tell you a thing that will make you wish yourself here. The small-pox, so fatal and so general amongst us, is here entirely harmless by the invention of ingrafting, which is the term they give it. There is a set of old women who make it their business to perform the operation every autumn, in the month of September, when the great heat is abated. People send to one another to know if any of their family has a mind to have the small-pox; they make parties for this purpose, and when they are met (commonly fifteen together) the old woman comes with a nutshell full of the matter of the best sort of small-pox, asks what vein you please to have opened. She immediately rips open that you offer to her with a large needle (which gives you no more pain than a common scratch), and puts into the vein as much matter as can lie upon the head of her needle, and after that binds up the little wound with a hollow bit of shell; and in this manner opens four or five veins. . . . The children or young patients play together all the rest of the day, and are in perfect health to the eighth [day]. Then the fever begins to seize them, and they keep their beds two days, very seldom three. They have rarely above twenty or thirty [pock marks] in their faces, which never mark; and in eight days time they are as well as before their illness.

1. Why might Lady Montagu been so interested in the inoculation process she describes in her letter?

2. In a sentence, sum up the process Lady Montagu describes in the letter.

3. Why do you think Lady Montagu never got the credit she deserved for introducing inoculation against smallpox to the English?

4. If you were in Lady Montagu's place, would you have inoculated your son against smallpox? Why or why not?

CHAPTER TEST 3

AN AGE OF SCIENCE & REVOLUTIONS, 1600–1800

NAME _____ **DATE** _____

A. COMPREHENSION

Circle the letter of the best answer to each question.

1. Which group of boys was **not** part of the collection?
   a. nonbelievers
   b. Muslims
   c. Jews
   d. Christians

2. Which is the best description of the pages' training?
   a. solely religious
   b. solely secular
   c. varied depending on their interests and skills
   d. varied depending on the skills needed by the court

3. Why did the collection system produce better administrators than the European system did?
   a. People in the Ottoman Empire were natural administrators.
   b. Administering the Ottoman Empire was easier than administering European countries.
   c. The boys in the collection system came from various religions.
   d. The collection system trained people to do administrative work.

4. Muslims regarded the Quran as
   a. hard to memorize.
   b. perfect and necessary.
   c. very interesting.
   d. a book of tales.

5. Why was Islamic clergy against the study of astronomy and astrology?
   a. The Quran forbade them.
   b. They contradicted Islamic law.
   c. These sciences were too European.
   d. The clergy believed that only the Quran was worth of study.

6. Which feature was **not** essential in mosque architecture?
   a. a central dome
   b. a prayer niche
   c. a tower
   d. a tile roof

B. SHORT ANSWER

Answer each question with one or more sentences.

7. Why did Albanians consider Skanderbeg a hero?
   _____
   _____

8. According to Bobovi, why were the pages taught to memorize the Quran?
   _____
   _____

9. How did English architect Christopher Wren demonstrate how impressed he was with Muslim architecture?
   _____
   _____

C. ESSAY

On a separate piece of paper, write a few paragraphs explaining the life of a page in the sultan's palace.

CHAPTER 4

PEACOCKS AND THE POWER OF PACHYDERMS: THE WONDERS OF MUGHAL INDIA PAGES 60–72

FOR HOMEWORK

STUDENT STUDY GUIDE

pages 23–26

CAST OF CHARACTERS

Babur (BAH-buhr) founder of Mughal Dynasty in India

Akbar (AHK-bahr) **the Great** effective Moghul rulers, known for his religious tolerance, administrative ability, and sponsorship of the arts

Jahangir (juh-HAHN-geer) Akbar's son, rebelled against his father and assumed the throne at Akbar's death in 1605

Nur Jahan (NOOR-juh-HAHN) wife of sultan Jahangir and Empress of India who commissioned the building of great monuments

Shah Jahan Jahangir's son and successor who built Taj Mahal in memory of his wife Mumtaz Mahal

Mumtaz Mahal (muhm-TAHZ mah-HAHL) beloved wife of Shah Jahan who died young in childbirth and to whom the Taj Mahal was dedicated

Aurangzeb (oh-rahng-ZEHB) son of Shah Jahan and the last great Mughal emperor

CHAPTER SUMMARY

The Mughal dynasty comprised descendents of Turkish tribes that, under a leader named Babur, finally succeeded in moving south. Mughal emperors ruled India from 1526 to 1858. The warlike Mughal rulers fought with one another and attempted to spread their Muslim faith among the mostly Hindu Indians. The Mughals also traded cloth, spices, and other goods with countries in Europe and elsewhere and became wealthy. Some of that wealth supported magnificent works of art and architecture such as the Taj Mahal. Eventually the Mughal rulers became too weak to hold the empire together against independence-minded local princes, rebellious Hindus, and English administrators.

PERFORMANCE OBJECTIVES

▶ To describe the origins and functioning of the Mughal Dynasty in India
▶ To analyze the effects of Mughal leaders' Muslim religious beliefs
▶ To analyze works of art created under the Mughal rulers
▶ To compare and contrast various Mughal rulers
▶ To explain the causes of the fall of the Mughal empire

BUILDING BACKGROUND

Show students the photograph of the Taj Mahal on Student Edition page 70 and, if possible, other photographs of the building taken at different times of day. Let students try to identify the structure and explain the reason it was built. If necessary, explain that the Taj Mahal is arguably the most famous tribute to love in the world. Encourage students to speculate about what kind of personal qualities a ruler would have to possess to command the construction of such a magnificent building and what sort of society would be capable of producing it. Tell students that they will learn in this chapter who was behind the construction of the Taj Mahal and the great love that inspired it.

VOCABULARY

expedition a journey with a definite goal

intimidating filling with fear

outpost an outlying settlement

seclusion the state of being removed from others

sibling a brother or sister

revenue income

As needed, have students consult the glossary to define the following word: *caste*.

WORKING WITH PRIMARY SOURCES

Use a *Sourcebook* selection to add to students' understanding of a Mughal ruler discussed in this chapter of their text. Explain to students that the Mughal ruler Akbar, though Muslim as all Mughal rulers were, was astonishingly tolerant of other beliefs and had a keen interest in all religions. Read aloud the excerpt "Live and Let Live" on page 81 of *The Medieval & Early Modern World Primary Sources and Reference Volume* or make photocopies for students to read. Then discuss the passage. Have students consider what sort of mind Akbar had, the effect his beliefs might have had on his rule, and the point of view of the writer of these observations, Abd ul-Qadir Bada'uni.

READING COMPREHENSION QUESTIONS

1. What was the Mughal dynasty? (*a line of Muslim emperors who ruled India from 1526 to 1858*)
2. Who was Babur? (*the leader of a Turkish tribe that moved south and took power in India*)
3. How did the Mughal's faith differ from that of most Indians? (*The Mughals were Muslim; most Indians were Hindu.*)
4. Why weren't the Indians interested in buying cloth from the British East India Trading Company in the early 17th century? (*They liked their own beautiful cloth better.*)
5. What was unusual about Nur Jahan? (*Though a woman, she gained power. She made government appointments, collected taxes, constructed monumental buildings, and supported artists.*)
6. What did Aurangzeb do that changed the tone of the Mughal Empire, and how would you describe that change? (*Possible answer: He stopped building great monuments, shut down the production of Mughal art, and assigned secret police to monitor conduct and rule following. The tone of the Empire became increasingly intolerant and repressive.*)

CRITICAL THINKING QUESTIONS

1. What were two important differences between the religious beliefs of Muslims and Hindus in India during this period? (*Muslims believed in one god; Hindus believed in many. Hindus believed in the caste system, and Muslims did not.*)
2. How would you compare Akbar and Jahangir as people and as rulers? (*Possible answer: Akbar was peaceable until provoked and interested in developing industry and trade. Jahangir could be fair or amazingly cruel. In addition, he was inclined to excess drinking and drugs.*)
3. Was trade with the British a helpful development or a harmful one for the Mughal Dynasty? (*Possible answer: It was both helpful and harmful—helpful because it increased the Dynasty's wealth, harmful because it let the British establish administrative power in India.*)

SOCIAL SCIENCES

Science, Technology, and Society Ask students to compare the current definition of factory with the factories that the British established throughout India during the Mughal period. Encourage students to speculate about which group benefited more from these factories, the Indians or the British.

THEN and NOW

From the time it was built, the Taj Mahal has drawn visitors. The famed tomb of Mumtaz Mahal is one of the loveliest and most romantic buildings in the world. Clad in white marble, the onion dome, four minarets, and reflecting pool of the Taj Mahal glow orange at sunset and ghostly white in moonlight. Tourists can once again visit the Taj Mahal at night, and thousands of them do each year.

AN AGE OF SCIENCE AND REVOLUTIONS, 1600–1800

LINKING DISCIPLINES

Math Have students draw a plan of the Taj Mahal to scale. First they must research the monument to find out what its size and dimensions are. Then they have to figure out an appropriate scale. Finally, they can draw their plan on graph paper. Remind them to include a key that shows the scale of their drawing.

LITERACY TIPS

In addition to using the suggestions in the Supporting Learning and Extending Learning sections, refer back frequently to pages 16–19 for strategies and advice from a literacy coach.

READING AND LANGUAGE ARTS

Reading Nonfiction Ask pairs of students to study the map on page 61 of the Student Edition or on the blackline master on the opposite page together to make sure they understand all of the symbols that appear on the map, as well as the distance scale and compass rose.

Using Language Have students examine the spelling, syntax, and unusual words in the excerpt from *Travels in Europe and Asia, 1632*, by Peter Mundy. Have them list archaic spellings and their modern equivalents and define uncommon words. Initiate a discussion of spelling before the advent of dictionaries and how spellings become standardized these days.

WRITING

Expository Paragraph Ask students to write a one-paragraph description of one of the works of art or architecture they read about in this chapter. Encourage them to try to capture the magnificence of the work in their description.

SUPPORTING LEARNING

English Language Learners Have students read the chapter in three sessions, pages 60 to 62, 62 to 68, and 68 to 72. List the names of people and places they will encounter in each session on the board before they begin reading. Pronounce each name and explain who the person was or where the place was. Encourage students to jot down troublesome words and work together to figure out what they mean from context.

Struggling Readers Have students use a timeline graphic organizer (see reproducibles at the back of this guide) to help them understand which ruler did what and when he did it. Point out that the text moves back and forth in time and a timeline can help them understand the order of events.

EXTENDING LEARNING

Enrichment Let students find out more about the composition, size, and main purpose of the Mughal army. Encourage students to locate primary source descriptions and accounts. Have them demonstrate what they learned in writing or art.

Extension Ask small groups of students to work together to write a dialogue between Emperor Akbar and his rebellious son Jahangir. Encourage groups to choose a dramatic moment in the interactions between the two: Jahangir's attempt to take over Agra, Akbar's confining his son to his rooms in 1604, Akbar's passing power to Jahangir, or Jahangir's last meeting with Akbar before the latter's death.

LITERATURE CONNECTION

The following books will broaden students' knowledge of the Mughal Empire.

Findley, Ellison Banks. *Nur Jahn: Empress of Mughal India*. (New York: Oxford University Press, 1993). This biography details the life of one of the most powerful women in Indian history.

Schimmel, Annemarie. *The Great Empire of the Great Mughals: History, Art, and Culture*. London: Reaction Books, 2004. An examination of the cultural and artistic achievements of the Mughal Empire.

NAME _____ DATE _____

CHAPTER BLM 4
AN AGE OF SCIENCE & REVOLUTIONS, 1600–1800

Directions

Study the map. Then answer the questions.

1. What geographic barrier borders the northern part of the Mughal Empire?
_____
_____

2. Which four cities belonged to the Mughal Empire in 1605 but not to the Mughal territories in 1765?
_____
_____

3. Which city on the map did not belong to the Mughals or Aurangzeb?
_____
_____

4. Which city is on the border between the Mughals and Aurangzeb areas?
_____
_____

CHAPTER 4 BLM   AN AGE OF SCIENCE & REVOLUTIONS, 1600–1800   **47**

CHAPTER 4 BLM

AN AGE OF SCIENCE & REVOLUTIONS, 1600–1800

NAME   **DATE**

COUNT ROLAND'S LAST STAND

Directions

Read the excerpt from Jahangir's memoirs in which he wrote about his 1605 coronation. Then answer the questions.

> For forty days and forty nights I caused the . . . great imperial state drum to strike up, without ceasing, the strains of joy and triumph; and around my throne, the ground was spread by my directions with the most costly brocades and gold embroidered carpets.

From Jahangir, *Memoirs* (c. 1627)

1. What effect do you suppose Jahangir's coronation ceremony was intended to have on its audience?

2. Which aspect of the coronation impresses you the most?

3. What assumptions can you make about a state that produced a coronation ceremony like Jahangir's?

4. How do you think Jahangir felt about his coronation? Why do you hold that opinion?

NAME   **DATE**

A. COMPREHENSION

Circle the letter of the best answer for each question.

1. Which word does **not** describe the Mughal Dynasty?
   - a. Muslim
   - b. successful
   - c. expansionist
   - d. unimportant

2. Which emperor was the strictest Muslim?
   - a. Babur
   - b. Akbar
   - c. Jahangir
   - d. Aurangzeb

3. Why was Mughal cloth so popular in England?
   - a. It was durable.
   - b. It was colorful.
   - c. It was washable.
   - d. It was waterproof.

4. Why is Mumtaz Mahal remembered today?
   - a. She exercised considerable power.
   - b. She inspired the building of the Taj Mahal.
   - c. She was one of many wives of a Mughal emperor.
   - d. She died in childbirth.

5. Why did the English establish factories in Mughal India?
   - a. to manufacture goods
   - b. to weave cloth
   - c. to sell products
   - d. to store goods

6. What was the Taj Mahal?
   - a. a tomb
   - b. a house
   - c. a palace
   - d. a throne

B. SHORT ANSWER

Answer the questions.

Why were elephants so important to the Mughal army?

_____
_____
_____

C. ESSAY

In a few paragraphs, explain who the greatest Mughal emperor was, and why he was the greatest. Use a separate sheet of paper.

AN AGE OF SCIENCE & REVOLUTIONS, 1600–1800   CHAPTER 4 TEST   **49**

CHAPTER 5

MISSIONARIES, MAPS, AND MAGISTRATES WITH PINK PARASOLS: CHINA ENCOUNTERS MODERN SCIENCE   PAGES 73–88

FOR HOMEWORK

STUDENT STUDY GUIDE

pages 27–30

CHAPTER SUMMARY

Jesuit missionary Matteo Ricci traveled to China in 1600 and learned the country's language and cultural traditions. Missionaries introduced Chinese scholars to Western sciences and mathematics, which the missionaries hoped would attract the Chinese to the Christian religon. They had limited success. Contact between the East and the West led to important exchanges in cultural ideas.

PERFORMANCE OBJECTIVES

- To understand the goals and accomplishments of Jesuit missionaries in China
- To compare Chinese and European educations
- To identify Confucius and explain his importance to Chinese education
- To identify Emperor Zhu Yizhun and describe his reign
- To describe the porcelain trade between Europe and China and explain its significance

BUILDING BACKGROUND

Ask students to imagine that they are talking to someone who has time traveled to the present day from many centuries ago. Let students describe the educational system in the United States to the time traveler. To stimulate discussion, ask questions such as: Who attends school? What kinds of schools are there? How many years do students go to school? What do students study? Tell students that the system of education in China in the 1600s was quite different from their own. Suggest to students that as they read, they should think about the type of citizens classic Chinese education might produce.

VOCABULARY

motives needs or feelings that move people to action

barbarians those thought by people of another group to have a primitive civilization

reclusive preferring to be alone

audience a formal meeting

provisions stores of needed supplies, especially food

WORKING WITH PRIMARY SOURCES

Let students learn more about the United East India Company and the porcelain trade on the following website: *http://cityu.edu.hk/ccs/Newsletter/newsletter5/China.htm*. On this site they can examine many examples of Chinoiserie, the fascinating blend of European designs and exquisite Chinese porcelain discussed in this chapter of their book.

CAST OF CHARACTERS

Matteo Ricci (mah-TAY-o REE-chi) Jesuit priest known for his missionary activity in China and the introduction of Western science and mathematics to the Chinese.

Confucius (con-FYU-shus) great Chinese philosopher who emphasized respect for parents and other basic values

Zhu Yizhun (joo ee-jwun) Chinese emperor of the Ming Dynasty who ruled for 48 years, despite being a weak leader who neglected his duties

CHAPTER 5

READING COMPREHENSION QUESTIONS

1. What was Matteo Ricci's main goal when he went to China in 1600? (*to convert the Chinese to Christianity*)
2. Why was Ricci compelled to disguise his goal? (*The Chinese would not have let him into the country if they had known his actual goal.*)
3. How did Chinese men become magistrates? (*They became scholars who won the highest honors in examinations.*)
4. What were the Chinese beliefs about the earth and sky? (*They believed the earth was flat and square and that the heavens were like a canopy.*)
5. What kind of ruler was Emperor Zhu Yizhun? (*weak, unpredictable, reclusive, neglectful of his duties*)
6. Why did Pronk porcelain fail to make a profit? (*The cost for the Chinese porcelain was too great and it took too long to produce from drawing to finished product.*)

CRITICAL THINKING QUESTIONS

1. Which countries gained more from contact between them, European countries or China? (*Most students will choose China because of the country's access to Western scientific and mathematical ideas; some will choose the West because of Chinese ideas about universal education based on excellence and governments run by educated officials rather than aristocrats with no special abilities, as well as the many imported Chinese products.*)
2. What does the word *china* tell you about the porcelain trade with China? (*The porcelain trade was so important that the ceramics that made it up came to be named after the country of origin, China.*)
3. Why do you think Europeans preferred ceramics from China to the imitations produced in Delft and other European cities? (*Chinese ceramics were more attractive and more refined technically.*)

SOCIAL SCIENCES

Civics Have groups of students work together to research how people became magistrates in Europe during the 17th and 18th centuries and learn more about the same process in China. Have students discuss advantages and disadvantages of both systems.

READING AND LANGUAGE ARTS

Reading Nonfiction Have students choose a paragraph in the chapter that confused them or that they found difficult to read. Give each student a photocopy of the main idea map (see reproducibles at the back of this guide). Ask students to write the main idea at the center and at least four supporting details in the outer ovals. Encourage them to add as many ovals as necessary to include all the important details in the paragraph.

Using Language Have students list the words related to ships and sailing that appear in the chapter. How many of these words do they know? How many can they get an idea about from context? Let students use a dictionary to confirm their definitions from context.

THEN and NOW

Chinese porcelain, including the type known as Chinoiserie, is valued today just as much as it was when Europeans first collected it. Encourage students to look for examples of Chinoiserie in their homes, in antique stores, in museums, or in photographs on the Internet.

AN AGE OF SCIENCE AND REVOLUTIONS, 1600–1800

LINKING DISCIPLINES

Art Ask students to look at the 18th-century example of Pronk porcelain on page 88 or do research to find other examples. Then discuss how these Chinoiserie patterns designed by European artists in the 1700s showed things that appealed to their tastes such as family coats of arms, country scenes, and so on. Ask students to design contemporary Chinoiserie porcelain patterns. Challenge students to design china patterns that would appeal to current tastes.

LITERACY TIPS

In addition to using the suggestions in the Supporting Learning and Extending Learning sections, refer back frequently to pages 16–19 for strategies and advice from a literacy coach.

WRITING

Persuasive Paragraph   Ask students to write a few paragraphs in which they try to convince readers that the Jesuit priest Matteo Ricci was one of the Europeans who most influenced relations between China and the West during the 16th and 17th centuries. Encourage them to discuss not only Ricci's accomplishments but also the traits he possessed that helped him accomplish them.

SUPPORTING LEARNING

English Language Learners   Pair English language learners with native English speakers. Have pairs take turns reading the chapter paragraph by paragraph. Let the students whose first language is English define words or explain idiomatic expressions that present problems to the English language learners.

Struggling Readers   Have students jot down challenging words from the chapter. Then have them reread each sentence that contains the challenging word and see whether any meanings become more clear. Encourage students to use context to figure out approximate meanings and then check their understanding by using a dictionary and a thesaurus. Students should focus on those words with meanings that are crucial to understanding important passages.

EXTENDING LEARNING

Enrichment   Let students investigate the shipwreck of the *Geldermalsen*. Encourage them to find out when the shipwreck was discovered and how divers explored it. Have students find out exactly what was recovered from the *Geldermalsen* and where these items are today.

Extension   Pairs of students can write and perform dialogues in which one partner plays the part of a Chinese magistrate and the other partner the part of a European magistrate. The magistrates should discuss how they came to hold their jobs and defend that system. An audience can decide which magistrate presented the most convincing argument.

NAME   **DATE**

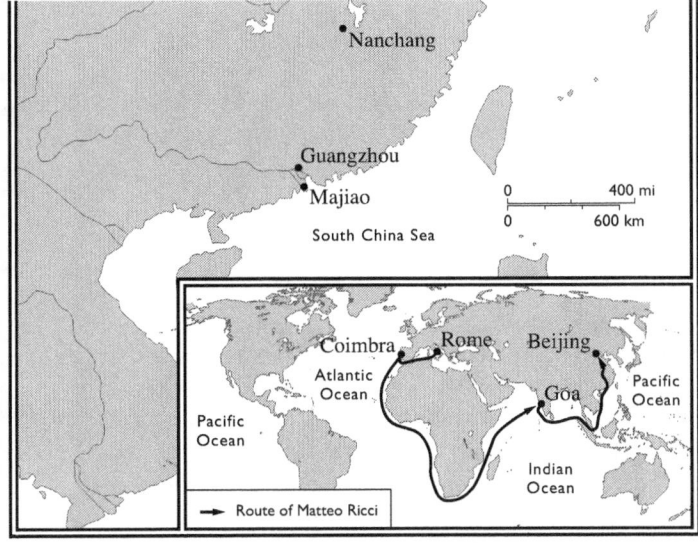

Directions

Look at the map at the left. Then answer the questions.

Size: 24p x 32p8

1. Explain why there are two different maps pictured.
_____
_____

2. What was Matteo Ricci's starting point and and what was his final destination?
_____
_____

3. Estimate the number of miles between the Chinese city that is furthest south and the only city located on the Yangzi River.
_____
_____

4. Explain why Ricci might have chosen to travel by water around Africa rather than go overland.
_____
_____

CHAPTER 5 BLM   AN AGE OF SCIENCE & REVOLUTIONS, 1600–1800   **53**

RULES TO LIVE BY

Directions

This excerpt is from *Articles of Instruction* by philosopher Zhu Xi in which he interprets the ideas of Confucius. You will also find it on pages 78–79 of the Student Edition. Read the passage and then answer the questions.

>Affection between parent and child;
>Righteousness between ruler and subject;
>Differentiation between husband and wife;
>Precedence between elder and younger;
>Trust between friends.

The above are the items of the Five Teachings. When Yao [the ancient sovereign ruler] and Shun appointed Hsieh to be Minister of Education and to set forth reverently the Five Teachings, it was precisely these teachings. Students should study these and nothing more. In studying, there is a proper sequence, which likewise involves five items, listed separately below:

>Study extensively, inquire carefully, ponder thoroughly, sift clearly, and practice earnestly.

The above is the proper sequence for studying. Studying, inquiring, pondering, and sifting are the means by which to probe [moral] principle. As to earnest practice, its essence is present in every step from self-cultivation on down to handling affairs and dealing with others, as follows:

>Be loyal and true to your every word, serious
>and careful in all you do.
>Curb your anger and restrain your lust; move
>toward the good and correct your errors.

The above are the essentials of self-cultivation.

>Accord with the righteous, do not seek profit;
>illuminate the Way, do not calculate the advantages.

The above are the essentials for handling affairs.

>Do not do to other what you do not want
>done to you. Whenever you fail to achieve
>your purpose, look into yourself.

The above are the essentials for dealing with others.

1. Based on the first five lines of the excerpt, how would you describe Confucius's ideal society as described by Zhu Xi?

2. Most educators and students today would not accept the statement that the Five Teachings represent everything that students should study. But what do you think about the sequence of study Zhu Xi sets out? Explain your answer.

3. What does the sentence "Do not do to others what you do not want done to you" mean? Have you ever heard a statement that is similar to this one? Explain.

4. Which values that you consider important are left out of Confucius's advice as transmitted by Zhu Xi?

NAME   **DATE**

An Age of Science & Revolutions, 1600–1800

A. COMPREHENSION

Circle the letter of the best answer for each question.

1. What did Matteo Ricci think would happen if he told the Chinese government the real reason he entered the country?
   a. He would have been forced to become a missionary.
   b. He would not have been allowed to enter the country.
   c. He would have been accepted and easily trusted.
   d. He would not have been able to find a place to live.

2. Why did Father Ricci learn Chinese?
   a. because he was commanded to
   b. as an aid in conversion
   c. because he loved learning
   d. to get along better in China

3. Chinese education was based on a series of
   a. grades.
   b. teachers.
   c. books.
   d. exams.

4. Why were Chinese scholars outraged when they first saw European world maps?
   a. China was not on the maps.
   b. The maps looked different from Chinese maps.
   c. Europe was in the middle of the maps
   d. China was smaller than they expected.

5. Why could the Jesuits predict the timing of an eclipse better than the Chinese?
   a. The Jesuits were smarter than the Chinese.
   b. The Jesuits were better educated than the Chinese.
   c. The Jesuits knew geometry and the Chinese did not.
   d. The Jesuits knew how to use telescopes and the Chinese did not.

6. Which statement is true of Pronk Porcelain?
   a. It dated to the time before trade with Europe.
   b. It was based on Chinese designs and porcelain.
   c. It made the United East India Company rich.
   d. It was a kind of Chinoiserie.

B. SHORT ANSWER

Complete each sentence with information from the chapter.

7. What was the *Geldermalsen*?

_____

_____

8. Why did Pronk Porcelain represent a new step in international trade?

_____

_____

C. ESSAY

On a separate piece of paper, write a few sentences explaining how Father Ricci got the Chinese interested in Christianity.

CHAPTER 6

THE SECRETS OF THE HEAVENS: NEW SCIENTIFIC THEORIES
PAGES 89–99

FOR HOMEWORK

STUDENT STUDY GUIDE
pages 31–33

CAST OF CHARACTERS

Ptolemy (TAH-luh-mee) Greek astronomer who lived in Egypt and wrote a book that summed up knowledge about the heavens and described an earth-centered system

Ibn al-Haytham (IH-bin ahl-hah-EE-thum) Muslim scholar who found flaws in Ptolemy's theories of planetary movements

Nicholas Copernicus (Kuh-PER-nih-kuhs) Polish mathematician who developed a sun-centered theory of the universe

Galileo Galilei (gah-luh-LAY-o gah-luh-LAY) Italian astronomer and mathmetician who used the telescope to study the stars

Tycho Brahe (TEE-ko BRAH-hay) Danish astronomer whose accurate observations formed the basis of Johannes Kepler's work

Johannes Kepler (YO-hahn-ess KEH-pler) German astronomer and mathematician whose three laws of planetary motion gave mathematical support to idea of a sun-centered universe

CHAPTER SUMMARY

For nearly fifteen centuries, Greek astronomer Ptolemy's book the *Almagest* was an important reference book for astronomers. However, scholars in the 11th century began to find mistakes in Ptolemy's earth-centered system. Copernicus's theory put the sun at the center of the universe. Galileo adopted Copernicus's theory, which angered the Catholic Church because the Bible described the earth as the center of the universe. But scientific support for sun-centered systems grew. Tyco Brahe was the greatest observer of astronomical phenomena of the time, and Johannes Kepler had the mathematical skill to analyze Brahe's data. At last astronomers had a strong mathematical argument for a sun-centered system. The work of Copernicus, Galileo, Brahe, and Kepler contributed to the birth of modern science.

PERFORMANCE OBJECTIVES

▶ To identify Ptolemy, describe his achievements, and analyze the flaws in his scholarship

▶ To explain the contributions to science of Copernicus, Galileo, Brahe, and Kepler

▶ To contrast views of the functioning of the universe held by scientists and the Church in the 16th and 17th centuries

BUILDING BACKGROUND

Let a volunteer demonstrate using balls or other round objects to show how the earth revolves as it rotates around the sun. Then have the class discuss whether this idea seems logical in light of common-sense daily observations of the earth and the sun. Help students appreciate how counter-intuitive this idea once was. Tell them that in this chapter they will learn how long it took for the idea of a sun-centered system to be accepted and why scientists struggled so hard not only to understand the solar system, but to convince people of the soundness of their ideas.

VOCABULARY

rotated turned around on a center

orbit the path of one heavenly body as it revolves around another

vengeance punishing in return for a wrong committed

fathom comprehend

heresy opinion or idea that varies from established Catholic beliefs

As needed, have students consult the glossary to define the following words: *astronomy*.

WORKING WITH PRIMARY SOURCES

The beginning of modern science was an exciting era. Any educated person with an inquiring mind and acute powers of observation could contribute to the store of scientific knowledge, and amateur scientists gathered together in scientific societies in London, Paris, and other cities to discuss their findings. Students can glimpse into this exciting period through the excerpt from Count Lorenzo Magalotti's *Travels of Cosmo, Grand Duke of Tuscany*, which is on page 109 of *The Medieval & Early Modern World Primary Sources and Reference Volume*. Have a volunteer read the selection aloud, or have students read photocopies. Then discuss the passage. Challenge students to speculate about the effect of academies like the one Magalotti describes and their heritage of intriguing items from faraway places.

READING COMPREHENSION QUESTIONS

1. What was Ptolemy's great achievement? (*He wrote the* Almagest, *in which he summed up the world's knowledge of astronomy.*)

2. How important was Ptolemy's work? How do you know? (*It was very important; it was the standard reference for nearly fifteen centuries.*)

3. What theory did Copernicus propose, and why did he think people would make fun of it? (*He proposed that the earth revolved around the sun; since this went against what people saw, he was afraid they would make fun of his theories.*)

4. What did the Church fathers think of Copernicus's work? Give evidence for your answer. (*They disagreed with his view and put the book in which he introduced it on their list of banned books, which Catholics were forbidden to read.*)

5. What did Galileo mean when he said: " . . . the intention of the Holy Spirit is to teach us how one goes to heaven and not how heaven goes"? (*He meant that people should not interpret the Bible literally but use it as a spiritual guide.*)

6. How would you sum up Kepler's contribution to astronomy? (*His three laws explained the movement of the planets mathematically and supported the argument for a sun-centered system.*)

CRITICAL THINKING QUESTIONS

1. Centuries before Ptolemy, Aristarchus suggested that the sun was the center of the universe and the earth rotated on its axis. Yet it was nearly twenty centuries before this idea was accepted. Why do you think it took so long? (*Possible answer: The idea went against what people saw, so it seemed outrageous. The Church believed the idea contradicted the Bible. A new way of conducting science based on observation had to be in practice.*)

2. Despite Galileo's and Copernicus's books being banned and Galileo renouncing the idea that the earth circled the sun, scientific exploration of the theory continued. Why? (*A sun-centered system explained what scientists observed and measured.*)

3. What did Kepler mean in the following quotation? Why do you or don't you agree with it? "We do not ask for what useful purpose the birds do sing, for song is their pleasure since they were created for singing. Similarly, we ought not to ask why the human mind troubles to fathom the secrets of the heavens." (*Kepler meant that trying to figure out how nature works is as natural to humans as singing is to birds. Students may agree or disagree with Kepler's view of human nature.*)

THEN and NOW

Early astronomers such as Copernicus, Brahe, and Kepler relied on what their eyes could see with the help of simple instruments. They would not recognize the telescopes, computers, and other sophisticated equipment astronomers use today.

AN AGE OF SCIENCE AND REVOLUTIONS, 1600–1800

LINKING DISCIPLINES

Math Let students prove Kepler's third law of planetary motion, which says that you arrive at the same number if you square the time it takes any planet to complete its orbit and then divide that number by the cube of its average distance from the sun. Ask a volunteer to demonstrate Kepler's third law for the class by doing the calculations on the board.

LITERACY TIPS

In addition to using the suggestions in the Supporting Learning and Extending Learning sections, refer back frequently to pages 16–19 for strategies and advice from a literacy coach.

SOCIAL SCIENCES

Science, Technology, and Society Have students work in small groups to find out more about the ideas of each of the astronomers discussed in this chapter. Each group should research a different scientist. Then have each group choose a representative to take the part of his or her group's scientist and explain and defend his views in a discussion with the other scientists.

READING AND LANGUAGE ARTS

Reading Nonfiction Have students make a timeline to clarify when new ideas and publications about astronomy were introduced. Give each student a photocopy of the timeline graphic organizer in the back of this guide. Ask students to note precise and approximate dates of the scientists' contributions. They can add boxes to the blackline master if they need to.

Using Language Ask each student to look up the origin of the name of one of the planets mentioned in the chapter. Ask: Which of the words originally came from Latin or Greek? Then have students describe what they learned about the word's origin to their classmates.

WRITING

Biographical Sketch Ask students to choose one of the scientists they read about in this chapter. Let them describe what the scientist was like and how his personality traits may have influenced his scientific achievements. Then, "bind" or place the biographical sketches together for the class "library corner" for all students to learn from and enjoy.

SUPPORTING LEARNING

English Language Learners To help students learning English understand the topic of the chapter, have the class discuss the meaning of the *heavens* in the title. Elicit that the word means what we see in the sky and beyond. Then have small groups read the first several paragraphs of the chapter aloud. Ask students to work together to define any words they don't understand. Have students read the remainder of the chapter silently, consulting with each other or using a dictionary to figure out the meanings of unfamiliar words.

Struggling Readers Have students read the chapter with a reading buddy. Students can read the chapter silently paragraph by paragraph. After each paragraph, pairs work together to sum up the main idea. Reading buddies can use photocopies of the main idea and details graphic organizer in the back of this Teaching Guide to do this, or they can simply jot down the main ideas and details on blank sheets of paper.

EXTENDING LEARNING

Enrichment Encourage students who are intrigued by the theory in Ptolemy's work that the heavenly bodies were powered by huge, clear, hollow balls to find out more about this and other early theories of planetary movement. Challenge them to figure out why these theories, which strike people as so outlandish today, seemed reasonable at the time they were posited.

Extension Have students write obituaries for the scientists and scholars discussed in the chapter. Challenge students to sum up each person's achievements in a short paragraph.

CHAPTER 6 BLM — An Age of Science & Revolutions, 1600–1800

NAME _____ DATE _____

RULES TO LIVE BY

Directions

This excerpt is from Galileo's confession, which he signed after an appearance before the Inquisition in 1633. You will also find it on page 95 of the Student Edition. Read the confession and then answer the questions.

> I, Galileo, son of the late Vincenzio Galilei of Florence, seventy years of age . . . swear that I have always believed, and will continue to believe all that the Holy Catholic and Apostolic Church holds, preaches, and teaches. . . .
>
> I have been judged strongly suspected of heresy, in having held and believed that the sun is motionless in the center of the world, and the earth is not the center and moves. . . .
>
> With sincere heart and unfeigned faith, I abjure, curse, and detest the above-named errors and heresies . . . I swear that in the future I will never again say or assert, orally or in writing, anything that might cause a similar suspicion about me.

1. In your opinion, did Galileo confess sincerely? Give reasons for your answer.

_____
_____
_____
_____
_____
_____
_____

2. Why was the Catholic Church so upset by Galileo's ideas about a sun-centered universe?

_____
_____
_____
_____
_____
_____
_____

CHAPTER 6 BLM

AN AGE OF SCIENCE & REVOLUTIONS, 1600–1800

NAME **DATE**

Directions

Read the quotation from Bernard le Bovier de Fontenelle, from his *L'Histoire du renouvellement de l'Académie royale des Sciences* (History of the Renewal of the Royal Academy of Sciences), 1702. Then answer the questions.

> There came on the scene a certain German, one Copernicus, who made short work of all those various circles, all those solid skies, which the ancients had pictured to themselves. The former he abolished; the latter, broke in pieces. Fired with the noble zeal of a true astronomer, he took the earth and spun it very far away from the centre of the universe, where it had been installed, and in that centre he put the sun, which had a far better title to the honour.

1. Fontenelle used figurative language to try to capture the enormity of Copernicus's achievement for readers. What are some examples?

2. How did Fontenelle feel about Copernicus's ideas? Why do you think so?

3. To what do the words "all those various circles, all those solid skies" refer?

4. How would you sum up this excerpt in one sentence?

NAME   **DATE**

AN AGE OF SCIENCE & REVOLUTIONS, 1600–1800

A. COMPREHENSION

Circle the letter of the best answer for each question.

1. What was the most important reason people clung for so long to the idea that heavenly bodies revolved around the earth?
   a. Their calculations agreed with this idea.
   b. Scripture from all religions agreed with this idea.
   c. Their rulers agreed with this idea.
   d. Common sense supported this idea.

2. What was the *Almagest*?
   a. a book about the movements of heavenly bodies
   b. a book about the orbit of the earth
   c. a book about the movements of the stars
   d. a book about the rotation of the earth

3. How influential was the *Almagest*?
   a. highly
   b. very
   c. fairly
   d. hardly at all

4. Why didn't Copernicus publish his theory of the earth's movements?
   a. He was too shy.
   b. He was afraid of ridicule.
   c. He couldn't find anyone to publish his work.
   d. He didn't want to go against his family's wishes.

5. What did Church fathers call Galileo's ideas of a sun-centered universe?
   a. mistakes
   b. heresy
   c. silliness
   d. abominations

6. On the observations of which astronomer did Kepler base his theories?
   a. Ptolemy
   b. Copernicus
   c. Galileo
   d. Brahe

B. IN YOUR OWN WORDS

Read the quotation from Johannes Kepler in a letter to Tübingen professor Michael Maestlin, referring to his first book, *The Secret of the Universe* (1595). Then rephrase it in your own words.

"I wanted to become a theologian, for a long time I was restless. Now, however, behold how through my effort God is being celebrated in astronomy."

_____
_____
_____
_____
_____
_____
_____

C. ESSAY

On a separate piece of paper, write an essay explaining the history of the important discoveries and ideas of the scientist discussed.

CHAPTER 7

THE TOOLBOX OF THE ENLIGHTENMENT: THE SCIENTIFIC REVOLUTION PAGES 100–115

FOR HOMEWORK

STUDENT STUDY GUIDE
pages 34–37

CAST OF CHARACTERS

Marcello Malpighi (mahr-CHEHL–o mahl-PEE-gee) Italian doctor who discovered capillaries and proved the link between arteries and veins

William Harvey British doctor who first correctly described how the heart pumps blood around the body

Gerhardus Mercator (jehr-AHR-duhs mer-KAY-ter) Flemish cartographer who developed a way to make maps more accurate, now known as the Mercator projection, in which parallels and meridians are shown as straight lines

René Descartes (ruh-NAY day-CART) mathematician and philosopher who proclaimed, "I think, therefore I am"

Francis Bacon British scientist who championed the scientific method and encouraged experimentation

Sir Isaac Newton British scientist who defined the three laws of motion, including the law of gravity

Joseph Priestley British clergyman and scientist who helped discover oxygen

CHAPTER SUMMARY

New tools such as the telescope, the microscope, and more accurate maps contributed to the Scientific Revolution. But the real revolution was the scientific method, which removed bias and allowed a more accurate picture of the world. René Descartes arrived at scientific truths through philosophy, mathematics, and physics. Francis Bacon's *The New Organon* emphasized the importance of scientific experimentation. Isaac Newton invented calculus, a new mathematics he used to describe objects that moved erratically. People began to believe that scientists could eventually explain all natural phenomena.

PERFORMANCE OBJECTIVES

- To describe new scientific instruments
- To describe the scientific method and explain its importance
- To analyze the contributions to science and to the Enlightenment of René Descartes, Francis Bacon, and Isaac Newton

BUILDING BACKGROUND

Ask students how they would test a simple idea such as the benefits to a certain plant of adding a particular nutrient to soil. When students suggest setting up an experiment to test this hypothesis, explain that people didn't always turn naturally to experiments that could be repeated to prove whether something was true or not. Add that the scientific method was a great breakthrough in thinking that arrived with the Enlightenment, which they will read about in this chapter.

VOCABULARY

infinite without limits

infinitesimal so small it cannot be measured

bias errors caused by inaccuracies

erratically inconsistently or irregularly

contemplative thoughtful or meditative

As needed, have students consult the glossary to define the following word: *meridian*.

WORKING WITH PRIMARY SOURCES

Read aloud to the class Immanuel Kant's "Answer to the Question: What Is Enlightenment?" which is on page 118 of *The Medieval & Early Modern World Primary Sources and Reference Volume*. Have a volunteer summarize Kant's definition of Enlightenment. Then discuss Kant's ideas. Ask students what they think of the motto "Have the courage to use your own understanding" and ask whether they agree with Kant that people should always think for themselves and never accept the dictates of any authority.

GEOGRAPHY CONNECTION

Interaction Ask students to look at the Mercator map on page 105 of their books. Then ask them to turn to page 106 to look at the world map. Have students compare the meridian lines on each of these maps. How are they different? How are they actually the same?

READING COMPREHENSION QUESTIONS

1. Why didn't people believe what they saw through such instruments as telescopes and microscopes at first? *(People thought they could only believe what they saw with their eyes.)*
2. How did the telescope help Galileo? Give an example. *(It helped him understand the universe; for example, he found out that the Milky Way was a cluster of stars.)*
3. Why were people more suspicious of the microscope than the telescope? *(They could think of practical uses for the telescope but not for the microscope.)*
4. What improvements did Gerhard Kremer, or Mercator, make in maps? *(He developed a way to represent a curved world on a flat map.)*
5. How did Descartes prove to himself that he existed? *(He realized that his ability to think proved that he existed.)*
6. What were Bacon's four idols and what did they mean? *(Idols of the Tribe, or common prejudices; Idols of the Cave, or prejudices unique to each person; Idols of the Market-Place; prejudices which stem from the limits of language; and Idols of the Theater, outdated ideas and false assumptions.)*

CRITICAL THINKING QUESTIONS

1. The author of the chapter writes of the scientific revolution, "It wasn't the answers that created a revolution; it was the questions." How do you explain what the author means? *(Possible answer: It was the scientific method consisting of observation, experimentation, and replicability that were important, not the specific subject of a particular experiment.)*
2. Why was Newton's invention of calculus so important? *(Possible answer: calculus let scientists easily describe mathematically objects that moved erratically. That permitted scientists to describe the movements of the planets and other aspects of the physical world and led to many other scientific discoveries.)*
3. Read Newton's first law. What is one thing that it explains? "Every body continues in its state of rest, or of uniform motion in a straight line, unless it is compelled to change that state by forces impressed upon it." *(Possible answer: Something that is moving keeps moving in a straight line unless something else affects it. The moon orbits the earth, for example, because gravity keeps it where it is.)*

SOCIAL SCIENCES

Science, Technology, and Society Let students use a telescope to observe the night sky or a microscope to observe a drop of pond water. Have them record their observations accurately and completely for a period of several days. Then have them compare results and discuss what using one of these instruments to see what people had never seen before must have been like for early scientists.

THEN and NOW

People have always been curious about aspects of nature from the heavens to the human body and observed them carefully. But it wasn't until the development and use of the scientific method that people were able to investigate natural phenomena in an orderly way, conduct experiments that could be repeated, and build on what other researchers discovered.

LINKING DISCIPLINES

Science Let students choose recent discoveries about the universe, for example, new theories about black holes. Have them research the discoveries and describe them to their classmates. Have students explain the importance of the new knowledge and answer their classmates' questions.

LITERACY TIPS

In addition to using the suggestions in the Supporting Learning and Extending Learning sections, refer back frequently to pages 16–19 for strategies and advice from a literacy coach.

READING AND LANGUAGE ARTS

Reading Nonfiction Give each student a photocopy of the main idea map graphic organizer in the back of this guide. Ask students to choose one scientist from the chapter. Have them write that person's name and a description of one of his important achievements in the center oval. In the surrounding ovals, ask students to write how this scientist accomplished the achievement written in the center oval. Urge students to use an additional blackline master if necessary

Using Language Have students locate and list several words in the chapter whose exact definitions are unclear to them but whose approximate meanings they can figure out from context. Encourage them to check the meaning of the words in a dictionary to discover how close their definitions were to the dictionary definitions.

WRITING

Journal Ask students to choose an exciting moment in the life of one of the scientists discussed in this chapter. For example, they might choose the first time Marcello Malpighi looked through the microscope to observe animals too small to be seen with the unaided eye. Have them write the journal entry the scientist might have made that day.

SUPPORTING LEARNING

English Language Learners Define and discuss critical concepts from the chapter such as *Enlightenment, scientific revolution,* and *scientific method* with students learning English. Then discuss the title and headings to make sure that everyone understands them. Next have students read the chapter, using sticky notes to mark any passages that they can't figure out. When students have finished reading the chapter, discuss the meaning of the words and passages that puzzled most of the students.

Struggling Readers Have students take notes on index cards as they read the chapter. Ask them to make an index card for each person mentioned in the chapter and summarize the person's contribution to science or the Enlightenment. Let students compare cards after they finish.

EXTENDING LEARNING

Enrichment Let students draw what they observe through a telescope or a microscope. Then have them label what they observed. Display students' drawings in the classroom.

Extension Ask pairs of students to write and perform a role-play for an audience of classmates. Students can write roles for a reporter and one of the scientists in this chapter. Have the reporter ask about the scientist's discoveries and why they are important. Urge the student playing the scientist to use what he or she knows of the scientist's personality as well as his achievements in the responses. Challenge pairs to make the interviews interesting—even funny—as well as informative.

NAME _____ **DATE** _____

USE YOUR BRAIN

Directions

Read Immanuel Kant's 1784 essay "Answer to the Question: What Is Enlightenment?" Then answer the questions about it.

> Enlightenment is man's emergence from his self-imposed nonage. Nonage is the inability to use one's own understanding without another's guidance. This nonage is self-imposed if its cause lies not in lack of understanding but in indecision and lack of courage to use one's own mind without another's guidance. *Dare to know! (Sapere aude.)* "Have the courage to use your own understanding" is therefore the motto of the Enlightenment.
>
> Laziness and cowardice are the reasons why such a large part of mankind gladly remain minors all their lives, long after nature has freed them from external guidance. They are the reasons why it is so easy for others to set themselves up as guardians. It is so comfortable to be a minor. If I have a book that thinks for me, a pastor who acts as my conscience, a physician who prescribes my diet, and so on—then I have no need to exert myself. I have no need to think, if only I can pay; others will take care of the disagreeable business for me. . . .
>
> Thus it is very difficult for the individual to work himself out of the nonage which has become almost second nature to him. He has even grown to like it, and is at first really incapable of using his own understanding because he has never been permitted to try it. Dogmas and formulas, these mechanical tools designed for reasonable use—or rather abuse—of his natural gifts, are the fetters of an everlasting nonage. The man who casts them off would make an uncertain leap over the narrowest ditch, because he is not used to such free movement. That is why there are only a few men who walk firmly, and who have emerged from nonage by cultivating their own minds. . . .
>
> The enlightenment requires nothing but *freedom*—and the most innocent of all that may be called "freedom": freedom to make public use of one's reason in all matters. Now I hear the cry from all sides: "Do not argue!" The officer says: "Do not argue—drill . . . !" Only one ruler in the world says: "Argue as much as you please, and about what you please, but obey!" We find restrictions on freedom everywhere. But which restriction is harmful to enlightenment? I reply: the public use of one's reason must be free at all times, and this alone can bring enlightenment to mankind.

1. Kant uses the word *nonage* in the essay, which he defines as "the inability to use one's own understanding without another's guidance." What are some words we might use today to describe this condition?

_____
_____
_____

2. What was Kant's purpose in this essay? Did he achieve it? Give reasons for your answer.

_____
_____
_____

3. According to Kant, why is using one's reason challenging? Why do you, or don't you, agree?

_____
_____
_____

BURNING BRIGHT

Directions

Read the quotation from Joseph Priestley's *Experiments and Observations on Different Kinds of Gases* (1776). Then answer the questions.

> Still, however, having no conception of the real cause of this phenomenon, I considered it as something very extraordinary. . . . I particularly remember my telling [a colleague] that I was myself perfectly satisfied of its being common air, as it appeared to be so by the test of nitrous air; though, for the satisfaction of others, I wanted a mouse to make the proof quite complete.
>
> On the 8th of this month I procured a mouse, and put it into a glass vessel, containing two ounce-measures of the air from mercurius calcinatus [mercury oxide, a red powder]. Had it been common air, a full-grown mouse, as this was, could have lived in it about a quarter of an hour. In this air, however, my mouse lived a full hour; and though it was taken out seemingly dead, it appeared to have been only exceedingly chilled; for, upon being held to the fire, it presently revived, and appeared not to have received any harm from the experiment.

1. Why were investigations of gases particularly challenging for early scientists?

2. Why did Priestley use a mouse to prove that the gas in the glass container was "common air"?

3. What was the result of Priestley's experiment, and what conclusions did he draw from it?

4. Is Priestley's experiment a good example of the scientific method? Why or why not?

NAME   **DATE**

A. COMPREHENSION

Circle the letter of the best answer for each question.

1. Which was **not** an activity people envisioned the telescope helping?
   a. fighting battles
   b. traveling
   c. doing medicine
   d. looking at the sky

2. What did Malpighi discover with the aid of his microscope?
   a. the heart
   b. veins
   c. arteries
   d. capillaries

3. What obstacle did Gerhard Kremer overcome with his new system for maps?
   a. showing the size of the world
   b. showing a round earth on a flat map
   c. showing what the world's climate was like
   d. showing all the important details on a small map

4. What was the basis of the Scientific Revolution?
   a. better education of scientists
   b. the scientific method
   c. experimentation
   d. new instruments and techniques

5. How did Descartes's education differ from traditional education of his time?
   a. Descartes read books other than the Bible.
   b. Descartes memorized more books than most students.
   c. Descartes did not have to study what didn't interest him.
   d. Descartes learned how to study rather than what to study.

6. There was only one thing that Descartes accepted as true. What was it?
   a. his existence
   b. science
   c. the earth
   d. mathematics

B. SHORT ANSWER QUESTIONS

7. Why didn't people trust what they could see in a telescope?

_____
_____
_____

8. What is a Mercator map and why was it important?

_____
_____
_____

C. ESSAY

On a separate piece of paper, write a few paragraphs about Sir Isaac Newton and his contributions to the world of science.

CHAPTER 8

BOLD IDEAS AND PRISON SENTENCES: THE LITERARY LIFE
PAGES 116–126

FOR HOMEWORK

STUDENT STUDY GUIDE
pages 38–40

CHAPTER SUMMARY

Through their writings, Voltaire and Montesquieu criticized the French government and Catholic Church. These writers argued for a republican form of government and religious freedom. Diderot organized and edited an all-encompassing encyclopedia, which also angered the government and Church because it criticized these institutions and made this information available to everyone. The ideas of these three men and many others set the stage for the French revolution.

PERFORMANCE OBJECTIVES

- To analyze the ideas of Voltaire, Montesquieu, and Diderot
- To describe the lives and works of Voltaire, Montesquieu, and Diderot
- To understand the effects of the works of Voltaire, Montesquieu, and Diderot on society

BUILDING BACKGROUND

Initiate a discussion with students about voting. Talk about the importance of voting to a democracy, voting patterns in the United States, and possible reasons for low voter turnout. Point out that in 18th-century France, the idea of a democracy in which citizens elect their leaders was an outrageous one; France was and had always been governed by a monarchy supported by the Catholic Church. Encourage students to consider as they read the chapter why the ideas of Voltaire, Montesquieu, and Diderot were so threatening to the status quo and the eventual effect their ideas might have had on people at that time.

VOCABULARY

crusaders people who fight for causes or against abuses
despoiled robbed
reform putting an end to abuse
censors people who examine books and other materials for moral and political content
parliament national representative group
random having no particular pattern
subtle hard to notice
corruption dishonesty

CAST OF CHARACTERS

François-Marie Arouet de Voltaire (vohl-TAIR) philosopher, novelist, and political essayist of the French Enlightenment

Baron de Montesquieu (bah-RON duh mon-teh-SKYUH) French political thinker and writer who proposed the separation of the powers of government

Denis Diderot (day-NEESS DEE-der-o) French writer and philosopher; editor-in-chief of the *Encyclopédie*

WORKING WITH PRIMARY SOURCES

Read aloud several or all of the following sayings to the class. Voltaire: "The true character of liberty is independence, maintained by force." "A little evil is often necessary for obtaining a great good." "I may disapprove of what you say, but will defend to the death your right to say it." Montesquieu: "Countries are well cultivated, not as they are fertile, but as they are free." "It is necessary from the very nature of things that power should be a check to power." Diderot: "Justice is the first virtue of those who command, and stops the complaints of those who obey." "Ignorance is less remote from truth than prejudice." Then ask volunteers to paraphrase the sayings to make sure everyone understands them. After that, let students explain why they agree or disagree with each one. As they read the chapter, students can decide how compatible the sayings of each person are with his beliefs and actions.

READING COMPREHENSION QUESTIONS

1. Why did Voltaire admire England so much? (*He felt that people were far freer in England than in France.*)
2. Why was Voltaire's work censored in France? (*It threatened the power of the monarchy and of the Catholic Church.*)
3. What was Montesquieu's purpose in his *Persian Letters,* and how did they help him achieve it? (*He wanted to criticize the government and the Church; the imaginary letters helped him do so indirectly through humor.*)
4. What important conclusion did Montesquieu arrive at from his study of history? (*that history is governed by causes rather than a random series of events*)
5. For Montesquieu republics were the fairest form of government. How did he believe a republic must function to succeed? (*A republic must have separation of powers.*)
6. What topics went into Diderot's encyclopedia? (*all knowledge in every field*)
7. In what way did the encyclopedia threaten the Church and government of France? (*It contained criticisms of the Church and monarchy, and it also put knowledge in the hands of everyone rather than reserving it for a privileged few.*)

CRITICAL THINKING QUESTIONS

1. What were the most important ways in which Voltaire, Montesquieu, and Diderot were similar? (*Possible answer: They were all brilliant, passionate writers from upper-class French families; each criticized the French monarchy and Catholic Church.*)
2. Though they tried, the French government and the Church couldn't prevent people from reading the works of Voltaire, Montesquieu, and Diderot. But what if they had been able to? What would have happened then? (*Possible answer: Because people had contact with other European countries, they would eventually have learned of these ideas.*)
3. Voltaire and Montesquieu used humor when they attacked French institutions in their writings. Why do you think they did this? (*Possible answer: Humor can be an effective tool for criticizing things or people by making them look absurd, ridiculous, or silly.*)

THEN and NOW

In 18th-century France, official censors were part of the government and had to approve every book before it could be published. The U.S. today has no official censors, but fact checkers and lawyers examine books carefully, especially nonfiction books on controversial subjects, before they are published.

LINKING DISCIPLINES

Music One of Voltaire's best-known literary works, *Candide*, was adapted as a musical comedy by Leonard Bernstein. Students might enjoy listening to a CD of Bernstein's *Candide* and sharing their reactions to the musical with each other. Encourage them to also talk about *Candide* as an expression of Voltaire's philosophy.

LITERACY TIPS

In addition to using the suggestions in the Supporting Learning and Extending Learning sections, refer back frequently to pages 16–19 for strategies and advice from a literacy coach.

SOCIAL SCIENCES

Civics Give students photocopies of the Venn diagram from the back of this guide. Let students use the diagram to compare and contrast the laws of England as Voltaire described them in his *Philosophical Dictionary* with the "divine right of kings," as it was practiced in France. Challenge them to think of ways in which the two systems were similar.

READING AND LANGUAGE ARTS

Reading Nonfiction Ask students to study the illustrations and captions in this chapter. Have volunteers talk about the kinds of information they get from illustrations that they don't get from text and the ways drawings and photographs help them understand what they read.

Using Language One common prefix is *in–*. Students will read two words with this prefix in the third paragraph of this chapter: *injustice* and *intolerance*. Encourage students to figure out what *in–* means from context. Then have them list some other common words with this prefix, for example, *inaccurate* and *insane*. Point out that the prefix *in–*. does not always mean "not." In some words, *in–* means "into." Mention that another prefix that means "not" is *im–*.

WRITING

Expository Essay Ask students to write a one-page essay in which they compare Diderot's *Encyclopédie* to modern encyclopedias. Have them use a comparison and contrast structure for their essay: an introduction, a conclusion, a paragraph of likenesses, and a paragraph of differences.

SUPPORTING LEARNING

English Language Learners Write idiomatic words and expressions from the chapter on the board, for example, "find trouble," "quick getaways," "wise-guy," "poke fun," and "wriggling out of work." Challenge students to explain what as many of these words and expressions mean as they can. Remind students to try to find the meaning of idioms from context. Have them to read on and gather the gist of a sentence or a passage even if they can't figure out a particular idiom. Encourage them to ask for help only when the meaning of an important sentence entirely escapes them.

Struggling Readers Have students use the main idea and details graphic organizer in the back of this guide to help them focus on important ideas about each of the great thinkers they read about in this chapter. Have them use this graphic organizer to sum up paragraphs four, nine, and fourteen.

EXTENDING LEARNING

Enrichment Invite students to use encyclopedias and other nonfiction resources to investigate the class structures in cities such as Tenoctitlan, London, Paris, and Beijing during the 15th and 16th centuries. Students can share their findings by preparing a chart that compares and contrasts the class structures of the cities.

Extension Have students take a point of view different from the one presented in this chapter. Ask them to imagine being a member of the royal family or a Church father. Have them describe their views of government and the Church and explain why their ideas are superior to those of Voltaire, Montesquieu, and Diderot.

NAME   **DATE**

Directions

Read the excerpt from *The Spirit of the Laws*, which Montesquieu wrote in 1748. Then answer the questions.

> On republican government and on laws relative to democracy
>
> In a republic when the people as a body have sovereign power, it is a *Democracy*. When the sovereign power is in the hands of a part of the people, it is called an *aristocracy*.
>
> In a democracy the people are, in certain respects, the monarchs; in other respects, they are the subjects . . . Therefore, the laws establishing the right to vote are fundamental in this government. Indeed, it is as important in this case to regulate how, by who, for whom, and on what issues votes should be cast, as it is in a monarchy to know the monarch and how he should govern. . . .
>
> There need not be much integrity for a monarchical or despotic government to maintain or sustain itself. The force of the laws in the one and the prince's ever-raised arm in the other can rule or contain the whole. But in a popular state there must be an additional spring, which is VIRTUE.

1. Why do you think Montesquieu felt he had to describe the differences among a monarchy, aristocracy, and republic so carefully?

_____
_____
_____
_____

2. What did Montesquieu mean when he wrote that, "In a democracy the people are, in certain respects, the monarchs; in other respects, they are the subjects"?

_____
_____
_____
_____

3. Montesquieu wrote that a democratic form of government has more integrity than a despotic government. Why did he believe this was true?

_____
_____
_____
_____

Directions

Read the quotations from Voltaire's *Philosophical Dictionary* (1764). Then answer the questions.

> The institution of religion exists only to keep mankind in order, and to make men merit the goodness of God by their virtue. Everything in a religion which does not extend toward this goal must be considered alien or dangerous.

> The sovereign . . . has no right to use coercion to lead men to religion, which in its nature presupposes choice and liberty.

1. How does Voltaire feel about religion? Give evidence to support your answer.

_____
_____
_____
_____
_____
_____

2. Do you agree with Voltaire's view of religion? Why or why not?

_____
_____
_____
_____
_____
_____

NAME   **DATE**

A. COMPREHENSION

Circle the letter of the best answer to each question.

1. What did Voltaire admire about England that was not true of France?
   a. There was more censorship of his writing.
   b. People who disagreed with the king were put in prison.
   c. The Catholic church held all the power.
   d. The people there spoke their minds.

2. Why was Voltaire sent to prison?
   a. He stole from the offering box in church.
   b. He threatened the French king.
   c. He wrote against the government and Church.
   d. He liked England better than France.

3. Who decided what could be published in France in Voltaire's time?
   a. the king
   b. the pope
   c. the people
   d. the censors

4. Why did Montesquieu write the *Persian Letters*?
   a. to tell the story of two Persian travelers in France
   b. to tell about his travels in Persia
   c. to tell about his life in an aristocratic family
   d. to criticize and poke fun at French and European customs

5. According to Montesquieu, which was not a type of political system?
   a. anarchy
   b. despotism
   c. monarchy
   d. republic

6. Why did government officials ban the *Encyclopédie*?
   a. It called for revolution.
   b. It was too hard to read.
   c. It attacked the religion and government.
   d. It taught people how to build dangerous machines.

B. SHORT ANSWER

The following phrases are important to the ideas in the chapter: "the divine right of kings" and "separation of powers." Explain what each means and decide whether the thinkers discussed in this chapter were likely to have agreed with it.

_____
_____
_____
_____
_____
_____

C. ESSAY

On a separate piece of paper write an essay comparing the three thinkers—Voltaire, Montesquieu, and Diderot—discussed in the chapter.

CHAPTER 9
RISING STARS: WOMEN IN THE ENLIGHTENMENT
PAGES 127–140

FOR HOMEWORK

STUDENT STUDY GUIDE
pages 41–43

CAST OF CHARACTERS

Caroline Herschel well-known astronomer of the 18th century

Sir William Herschel the brother of Caroline, also an astronomer, who discovered the planet Uranus

Madame Anne Thérèse de Lambert (tay-REHZ duh lahm-BARE) salon hostess who believed women should be educated

Jean-Jacques Rousseau French philosopher, political theorist and writer who wrote *The Social Contract*

Marie Thérèse Geoffrin salon hostess; financially supported the development of the French encyclopedia

Mary Wollstonecraft writer who wrote about women's struggles and advocated more rights and freedoms for women

Hannah More member of the Bluestocking Circle who wrote in favor of women's education

CHAPTER SUMMARY

During the 17th and 18th centuries, women began coming to the forefront of the social and intellectual scene. Wealthy women began to invite intellectuals to their homes to discuss important topics. Others spoke out in favor of the education of women and made advancements in the fields of literature and the sciences.

PERFORMANCE OBJECTIVES

▶ To identify some of the important women who lived during the Enlightenment
▶ To understand some of the contributions of women during the Enlightenment
▶ To explain the contributions of women to the intellectual and social advancements that occurred during the Enlightenment

BUILDING BACKGROUND

Ask students to discuss the contributions women make to society today; for example, women can be doctors, lawyers, teachers, and principals. Today women go to school and have careers just as men do. Explain that there was a time when girls were not allowed to go to school and women could not have jobs outside of the home. Have students imagine what society would be like if women could not receive an education or have careers.

VOCABULARY

Enlightenment an intellectual movement in 18th-century Europe that fostered greater knowledge and progressive thinking, based on science and facts over religion and superstition

typhus a bacterial disease characterized by high fever, delirium, rash, and stupor

astronomy the study of the stars

comet a celestial body that moves through space away from the sun

salon a regular gathering of intellectuals for the purpose of discussing and learning about new ideas

WORKING WITH PRIMARY SOURCES

Have students read the quotations found in the margins of the chapter. Ask them to note whom each quotation is from. Then discuss how the words of these people represent the new role that women were taking in the intellectual discussions of the time.

READING COMPREHENSION QUESTIONS

1. What were some of the challenges Caroline Herschel had to face in her life? *(She was disfigured from smallpox, had stunted growth from typhus, and was not allowed an education because she was a girl.)*

2. How did William Herschel help his sister? *(He took her with him on his travels and taught her about astronomy and how to make and use telescopes.)*

3. What were the responsibilities of the salon hostesses? *(They decided who would be invited and what topics would be discussed. They encouraged opposing ideas but helped to keep the discussion civil.)*

4. How was Marie Thérèse Geoffrin different from the other salon hostesses of her time? *(Her education had been more limited than that of other hostesses. She said that her entire education came from the meetings in her salon.)*

5. What did Mary Wollstonecraft think about the education of girls? *(She believed that educating girls would make them more independent and able to be part of the world.)*

CRITICAL THINKING QUESTIONS

1. Why were the salons important? *(The salons offered a place for people to go to discuss important topics. They also provided a place where women could participate in these discussions.)*

2. How do you think the women discussed in the chapter may have impacted the lives of all women of their time? *(Possible answer: The women in the chapter were among the first to show that women were capable of having intellectual conversations about important topics of the day. They provided a place where women could be taken seriously and could increase their knowledge of the world.)*

SOCIAL SCIENCES

Civics Have students explore the rights of women in 17th-and 18th-century Europe. Encourage them to think about the rights people have today, such as voting and owning property, and to find out if women during the Enlightenment had these rights.

READING AND LANGUAGE ARTS

Reading Nonfiction Have students preview the chapter by looking at the title, pictures, graphic aids, and sidebars. Have them create a two-column chart with questions they have from their preview that they think might be answered in the chapter in the first column. For example, some questions might be: *Who were some of the important women of the Enlightenment? What role did these women have in the Enlightenment? Where did these women live?* Then have students answer these questions in the second column as they read.

Using Language The women who hosted salons had strict rules for the discussions that took place. They wanted everyone to understand the speakers and encouraged them to speak in a straightforward tone. They did not allow foul language or language that would cause others to become upset, even when people disagreed with the speakers. Have students list some phrases that the people at the salons might have used to politely state that he or she did not agree with what the other person was saying.

THEN and NOW

During the Enlightenment, the salons were a place where people could communicate about important issues of the time. Today, people have many other methods for communicating about the same types of issues such as politics and philosophy. People can have intellectual conversations with people on the Internet or over the phone. People can hear about important topics on television news programs or listen to them on the radio.

LINKING DISCIPLINES

Health Smallpox and typhus were diseases that afflicted many people before vaccinations were found to stop these diseases from spreading. Have students research the causes, symptoms, and effects of these diseases.

WRITING

Ship's Log Ask students to imagine they are reporters assigned to interview one of the women from the chapter. Have them write *who, what, why, when,* and *how* questions they would ask that person. Then, using what they have learned from the chapter, have them write the answers to the questions.

SUPPORTING LEARNING

English Language Learners Ask students to find examples of adverbs and adjectives in the chapter. Have them write down five examples of each and use each one in a sentence. Then have students explain how each adverb or adjective helps to make the ideas in the chapter clearer. Review with students that adverbs are words that describe verbs, or action words, and adjectives are words that describe nouns.

Struggling Readers Have students use the main idea map graphic organizer from the back of this guide to organize the ideas from the chapter. Ask them to write *Women of the Enlightenment* in the large circle and then, in the detail circles, write the names of the important women mentioned in the chapter and the contributions they made.

EXTENDING LEARNING

Enrichment Caroline Herschel was an important woman in the field of astronomy. Ask students to research Caroline Herschel and create a timeline of the important events in her life.

Extension Have small groups choose a topic of the day. The topic can be an issue in the news or politics, or another topic of interest that can have differing viewpoints. The small groups can then hold their own salons. Each group may choose to have a hostess or host to lead the discussion. Students should be reminded to follow the same rules of decorum as those of the original salons. If a student should disagree with what someone else is saying, he or she may use one of the phrases the class suggested during the *Using Language* activity.

LITERACY TIPS

In addition to using the suggestions in the Supporting Learning and Extending Learning sections, refer back frequently to pages 16–19 for strategies and advice from a literacy coach.

Directions

Read the quotations below. Then answer the questions that follow.

> Women fill the intervals of conversation and of life, like the padding that one inserts in cases of china; they are valued at nothing, and [yet] everything breaks without them.
> —Suzanne Necker (1777)

> Let not men then in the pride of power, use the same arguments that tyrannic kings and venal ministers have used, and fallaciously assert that woman ought to be subjected because she has always been so.
> —Mary Wollstonecraft (1792)

1. To what does Necker compare women?

2. What does Necker mean by this comparison?

3. What is Wollstonecraft's argument about the treatment of women?

4. What is similar about the meaning of these two quotes?

An Age of Science & Revolutions, 1600–1800 NAME DATE

Directions

Read the passage below, written from Hannah More's *Strictures on the Modern System of Female Education* (1799). Then answer the questions that follow.

> The profession of ladies, to which the bent of their instruction should be turned, is that of daughters, wives, mothers and mistresses of families. They should be therefore trained with a view to these several conditions and be furnished with a stock of ideas, and principles, and qualifications, and habits ready to be applied and appropriated, as occasion may demand, to each of these respected situations: for though the arts which merely embellish life must claim admiration; yet when a man of sense comes to marry, it is a companion whom he wants, and not an artist. It is not merely a creature who can paint, and play, and dress and dance; it is a being who can comfort and counsel him; one who can reason, and reflect, and feel, and judge, and act, and discourse, and discriminate; one who can assist him in his affairs, lighten his cares, soothe his sorrows, purify his joys, strengthen his principles, and educate his children.
>
> The chief end to be proposed in cultivating the understanding of women, is to qualify them for the practical purposes of life . . . A lady studies, not that she may qualify herself to become an orator or a pleader; not that she may learn to debate, but to act. She is to read the best books, not so much to enable her to talk of them, as to bring the improvements which they furnish, to the rectification of her principles, and the formation of her habits. The great uses of study are to enable her to regulate her own mind, and to be useful to others.

1. What is it that More is arguing men are looking for in a wife?

2. How is this idea different from what she thinks society is saying about what a woman should provide?

3. What does More think is a woman's true responsibility?

NAME _____ DATE _____

AN AGE OF SCIENCE & REVOLUTIONS, 1600–1800

A. COMPREHENSION

Circle the letter of the best answer to each question.

1. All of the following were challenges that Caroline Herschel faced as a child **except**
   a. her mother would not let her go to school.
   b. she was disfigured by smallpox.
   c. her growth was stunted by typhus.
   d. her brother, William, was unkind to her.

2. Caroline Herschel is an important figure in history because
   a. she was the first woman to discover a comet.
   b. she knew how to make a telescope.
   c. she had comets and planets named after her.
   d. she met with many important scientists and mathematicians.

3. The salons were intended as a place where all of the following could take place **except**
   a. women and men could discuss philosophy and politics.
   b. new ideas could be exchanged.
   c. controversial plays could be performed.
   d. the movement of the Enlightenment could be stopped.

4. The guests of Marie Thérèse Geoffrin's salon are responsible for which important contribution?
   a. the French *Encyclopédie*
   b. the reflecting telescope
   c. *The Social Contract*
   d. *A Vindication of the Rights of Women*

5. Mary Wollstonecraft put herself at the forefront of the Enlightenment with her idea that
   a. women should be kept in their place.
   b. women's education should make them independent.
   c. people should do what makes them happy.
   d. a person has a right to use reason and rationality.

B. INTERPRETING PRIMARY SOURCES

Read this quote from Mary Wollstonecraft. Then rephrase it in your own words.

> How many women thus waste life away the prey of discontent, who might have practiced as physicians, regulated a farm, managed a shop, and stood erect, supported by their own industry, instead of hanging their heads surcharged with the dew of sensibility, that consumes the beauty to which it at first gave lustre.

_____
_____
_____
_____
_____

C. ESSAY

On a separate piece of paper, write an essay describing the salons and the contributions they made to society.

CHAPTER 10

HEADS ROLLING: DEMOCRACY AND THE CONSENT OF THE PEOPLE PAGES 141–152

STUDENT STUDY GUIDE pages 44–46

CAST OF CHARACTERS

Hugo Grotius (GROH-shee-us) Dutch man who was imprisoned for trying to bring religious peace to Holland and later wrote *The Laws of War and Peace* in which he defines a "just war"

King Charles I English king who closed down Parliament in order to give himself more power and was eventually executed

Oliver Cromwell Puritan leader who wanted a simpler approach to religion and pushed for the execution of King Charles I

John Locke English philosopher who wrote *Two Treatises of Government* and believed that people should be free to practice whatever religion they should choose

CHAPTER SUMMARY

Hugo Grotius, King Charles I of England, and John Locke were three important people of the 1600s. Grotius spoke out about what is considered a "just war" and suggested reasons that would justify a war. King Charles I of England was beheaded because he did not want to have to answer to Parliament. Locke believed that people should have the right to their religion, which led to later ideas about separation of church and state. Differences in religious beliefs and the interaction of religion and government also contributed to the conflicts of the time.

PERFORMANCE OBJECTIVES

- ▶ To identify three important people in the development of democracy
- ▶ To understand the risks that some people in history took to speak out against the status quo
- ▶ To explain the steps involved in a government's movement toward democracy

BUILDING BACKGROUND

Ask students to name some people in history who were imprisoned or even killed for their beliefs, for example, Martin Luther King, Jr., Jesus Christ, Nelson Mandela, Cesar Chavez, and Rosa Parks. Then have students discuss the contributions these people made and how their sacrifices led the way for change.

VOCABULARY

inquisitors people who ask questions

pardon the excusing of an offence without punishment

treason the illegal act of trying to overthrow the government

prodigy a highly talented child

negotiation the act of dealing with a problem by finding a compromise

As needed, have students consult the glossary to define the following word: *scaffold*.

WORKING WITH PRIMARY SOURCES

Use the quote from John Locke on page 149, first paragraph, to point out his idea that people should be free to practice the religion they choose. Have students discuss how this idea is present in the laws of the United States. Students can give examples of how church and state are separate. Students may mention that there is no prayer in public schools or that there has been some controversy regarding the mention of God in the Pledge of Allegiance.

80 CHAPTER 10

GEOGRAPHY CONNECTION

Location The Hague in the Netherlands has long been a political power. Today it is a business center of Europe and the location of the International Court of Justice. Help students find The Hague on a map of Europe. Students can also go online to find out more about the history, culture, and politics of The Hague. One helpful website is *www.thehague.nl*.

READING COMPREHENSION QUESTIONS

1. Why was Hugo Grotius brought to trial? (*He was accused of high treason because he tried to get different religious groups to get along.*)
2. According to Grotius, what made a "just war"? (*need for defense, to recover lost territory or monetary payments, or to punish for an injury suffered*).
3. Why was King Charles I of England beheaded? (*Parliament was already unhappy with the King for his abuse of their position of rule. Therefore, they finally agreed when Oliver Cromwell pushed for the death sentence because he wanted religion to be simplified.*)
4. What were John Locke's beliefs about a person's religion? (*Locke believed that no one should be forced to have a religion he did not want. People should be free to have any religion they want.*)
5. What did John Locke's *Two Treatises on Government* cause? (*His writings led to the revolutionary movements in America and France.*)

CRITICAL THINKING QUESTIONS

1. Of the three major characters mentioned in the chapter, which one do you think was the most influential in the way we think about religion and government today? (*Possible Answers: Grotius's ideas about "natural laws" form an international standard for conduct between nations, even those that subscribe to different religions. Locke's ideas about the separation of church and state remain as an important part of the United States government.*)
2. How did John Locke's ideas influence the writing of the Declaration of Independence of the United States? (*The Declaration of Independence is based on the ideas that people have the right to disagree with the government and change it. They also have the right to practice any religion they want. And they have the right to choose their own leaders.*)

SOCIAL SCIENCES

Civics Draw students' attention to the fact that Hugo Grotius was imprisoned for his beliefs that people of different religions should get along. At that time, people did not have the freedom to speak out against or question the government. Today, freedom of speech is one of the fundamental rights of the citizens of the United States. Encourage students to discuss some of the ways that Americans make their voices heard when they disagree with the government, such as petitions, letters to political leaders, etc. They may also like to mention the people discussed during the Building Background section of this lesson.

THEN and NOW

In the 1600s, people risked imprisonment and even death if they spoke out against or questioned the government. Today in the United States, people have the right to protest what the government does or to take an active roll in decisions the government makes.

AN AGE OF SCIENCE AND REVOLUTIONS, 1600–1800

LINKING DISCIPLINES

Arts–Drama Review the main events in each of the sections of the chapter. Then ask students to work in small groups to create a play in which they act these events out. Students can perform their plays for each other.

READING AND LANGUAGE ARTS

Reading Nonfiction Explain that the chapter is organized into three sections. Each section focuses on a different person. Have students make a three-column chart. At the top of each column, have students write the main idea of one of the sections. Then below each of these headings, students can write a few details to support the main idea at the top of the column.

Using Language Throughout the chapter the author asks questions to keep the reader's interest. Have partners find some of these questions and discuss how these questions affect their reading. Do the questions make them want to keep reading? Are there answers for these questions?

WRITING

News Article Ask students to imagine they are reporters sent to write a news article about the arrest, trial, and escape of Hugo Grotius. Students may choose to include opinions of Dutch citizens of the time.

SUPPORTING LEARNING

English Language Learners In small groups, have students make a three-column chart with the name of the three important characters from the chapter. Then ask students to make a list of adjectives in the appropriate column that describe each character.

Struggling Readers In small groups, have students read sections of the text to each other and ask each other questions about what they read.

EXTENDING LEARNING

Enrichment Have partners look through sections of the United States Constitution to find connections to the ideas of John Locke as stated in the chapter.

Extension Have pairs of students write what they think may have been the speech that King Charles I of England made just before his death. One student can then read the speech to the class.

LITERACY TIPS

In addition to using the suggestions in the Supporting Learning and Extending Learning sections, refer back frequently to pages 16–19 for strategies and advice from a literacy coach.

NAME   **DATE**

An Age of Science & Revolutions, 1600–1800

Directions

The Edict of Nantes guaranteed that Protestants could live and practice their religion in France freely. However, in 1685, this Edict was revoked, or taken back. The passage below is the Revocation of the Edict of Nantes. Read the passage with a partner. Then answer the questions.

> Be it known that . . . we have, by this present perpetual and irrevocable edict, suppressed and revoked, and do suppress and revoke, the edict of our said grandfather, given at Nantes in April, 1598, in its whole extent . . .
>
> We forbid our subjects of the R.P.R. [so-called Reformed Religion] to meet any more for the exercise of the said religion in any place or private house, under any pretext whatever. We likewise forbid all noblemen, of what condition soever, to hold such religious exercises in their houses or fiefs, under penalty to be inflicted upon all our said subjects who shall engage in the said exercises, of imprisonment and confiscation.
>
> We enjoin all ministers of the said R.P.R., who do not choose to become converts and to embrace the Catholic, apostolic, and Roman religion, to leave our kingdom and the territories subject to us within a fortnight of the publication of our present edict. . . . We forbid private schools for the instruction of children of the said R.P.R., and in general all things whatever which can be regarded as a concession of any kind in favor of the said religion.
>
> As for children who may be born of persons of the said R.P.R., we desire that from henceforth they be baptized by the parish priests. We enjoin parents to send them to the churches for that purpose, under penalty of five hundred livres fine. . . .

1. According to the Revocation of the Edict of Nantes, what were Protestants no longer allowed to do?

2. If Protestant ministers did not convert to Catholicism, what did they have to do?

3. What did the revocation mean for the children of Protestants?

4. What is your opinion of the Revocation of the Edict of Nantes? Explain.

CHAPTER 10 BLM
AN AGE OF SCIENCE & REVOLUTIONS, 1600–1800

WISH YOU WERE HERE

Directions

Read the passage below from *The English Declaration of Rights*, 1689. Then answer the question that follows.

[1.] That the pretended power of suspending of Lawes or the execution of Lawes by Regall Authority without Consent of Parliament is illegall.

[2.] That the pretended power of dispensing with lawes or the Execution of lawes by regall authority as it has been assumed and exercised of late is illegall . . .

[4.] That levying of money for or to the use of the Crowne by pretence of Prerogative without Grant of Parliament for longer time or in other manner, than the same is or shall be granted is illegall.

[5.] That it is the right of the Subjects to petition the King and all Commitments and prosecutions for such petitioning are illegall.

[6.] That the raiseing or keeping a Standing Army within the Kingdom in time of Peace unlesse it be with consent of Parliament is against Law.

[7.] That the Subjects which are Protestants may have Armes for their defence Suitable to their Condition and as allowed by Law.

[8.] That Elections of Members of Parliament ought to be free.

[9.] That the freedome of Speech and debates or proceedings in Parliament ought not to be impeached or questioned in any Courte or place out of Parliament.

[10.] That excessive Bayle ought not to be required nor excessive fynes imposed nor cruel and unusuall Punishments inflicted.

[11.] That Jurors ought to be duely impannelled and returned and Jurors which passe upon men in tryalls for high Treason ought to be freeholders …

[13.] And that for redress of all grievances and for the amending, strengthening and preserving of the Lawes, Parliaments ought to be held frequently.

IN YOUR OWN WORDS

Choose five of the rights listed above and write them on the lines below in your own words.

NAME   **DATE**

A. COMPREHENSION

Circle the letter of the best answer for each question.

1. All of the following are true of Hugo Grotius **except**
   a. he asked for a pardon.
   b. he was imprisoned for high treason.
   c. he wanted to help solve the problem of conflict between people of different religions.
   d. he escaped from prison.

2. Which of the following is **not** a reason for a "just war" according to Grotius?
   a. need for defense against threat of injury
   b. to recover what is legally due
   c. having different religious beliefs
   d. to punish for an actual injury suffered

3. King Charles I of England closed down Parliament because
   a. Parliament would not give him money or impose taxes when he asked.
   b. Parliament was made up of people from different religions.
   c. he wanted to force Scotland to share his ideas.
   d. he wanted to start a civil war.

4. John Locke believed that all men are free to do as they wish as long as they
   a. believe that their rulers held their positions by God's command.
   b. do not harm others.
   c. sacrifice their freedom of religion.
   d. give up their right to own property.

5. Which of Locke's ideas was behind the U.S. Declaration of Independence?
   a. People should give up some liberties for the good of the community.
   b. People should be free to practice their own religions.
   c. All men are free.
   d. When the government is not based on the consent of the majority, it has taken control unlawfully.

B. SHORT ANSWER

6. What actions by King Charles I and Parliament led to his death?

7. How did John Locke's ideas impact the new American government?

C. ESSAY

On a separate piece of paper, explain the ideas of Hugo Grotius in terms of how he thought nations should behave.

NAME   **DATE**

Directions
Answer each of the following questions. Use additional paper if necessary

1. Write a paragraph comparing and contrasting Bartholomew Gosnold's two voyages to the New World.

2. Adam Smith became famous for his influential book, *The Wealth of Nations*, which was published in the revolutionary year of 1776. Write a paragraph or two summarizing the book's ideas about trade.

3. Write a paragraph or two describing the *devshirme*, the "collection" system, and explaining how it benefited the Ottoman Empire.

4. Write a paragraph explaining the significance of elephants to the rulers of Mughal India.

5. Write a paragraph explaining why missionaries such as Matteo Ricci and other Jesuit priests had such a difficult time converting the Chinese to Christianity during the 16th and 17th centuries.

NAME   **DATE**

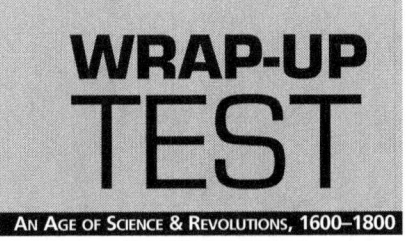
AN AGE OF SCIENCE & REVOLUTIONS, 1600–1800

6. In one to three paragraphs, describe how the discoveries of Copernicus, Galileo, and Kepler contributed to the birth of modern science.

7. Write a paragraph explaining why the Scientific Revolution was most importantly a revolution in thinking.

8. Write a one-paragraph explanation of this quote from Voltaire's *Philosophical Dictionary* and describe why quotations such as this were so revolutionary. "The sovereign . . . has no right to use coercion to lead men to religion, which in its nature presupposes choice and liberty."

9. In a paragraph or two, describe Mary Wollstonecraft's ideas about women and the way they should be educated.

10. Write several paragraphs explaining why John Locke's ideas in *Two Treatises of Government* were so revolutionary.

SCORING RUBRIC

The reproducibles on the following pages have been adapted from this rubric for use as handouts and a student self-scoring activity, with added focus on planning, cooperation, revision and presentation. You may wish to tailor the self-scoring activity—for example, asking students to comment on how low scores could be improved, or focusing only on specific rubric points. Use the Library/Media Center Research Log to help students focus and evaluate their research for projects and assignments.

As with any rubric, you should introduce and explain the rubric before students begin their assignments. The more thoroughly your students understand how they will be evaluated, the better prepared they will be to produce projects that fulfill your expectations.

	ORGANIZATION	CONTENT	ORAL/WRITTEN CONVENTIONS	GROUP PARTICIPATION
4	• Clearly addresses all parts of the writing task. • Demonstrates a clear understanding of purpose and audience. • Maintains a consistent point of view, focus, and organizational structure, including the effective use of transitions. • Includes a clearly presented central idea with relevant facts, details, and/or explanations.	• Demonstrates that the topic was well researched. • Uses only information that was essential and relevant to the topic. • Presents the topic thoroughly and accurately. • Reaches reasonable conclusions clearly based on evidence.	• Contains few, if any, errors in grammar, punctuation, capitalization, or spelling. • Uses a variety of sentence types. • Speaks clearly, using effective volume and intonation.	• Demonstrated high levels of participation and effective decision making. • Planned well and used time efficiently. • Demonstrated ability to negotiate opinions fairly and reach compromise when needed. • Utilized effective visual aids.
3	• Addresses all parts of the writing task. • Demonstrates a general understanding of purpose and audience. • Maintains a mostly consistent point of view, focus, and organizational structure, including the effective use of some transitions. • Presents a central idea with mostly relevant facts, details, and/or explanations.	• Demonstrates that the topic was sufficiently researched. • Uses mainly information that was essential and relevant to the topic. • Presents the topic accurately but leaves some aspects unexplored. • Reaches reasonable conclusions loosely related to evidence.	• Contains some errors in grammar, punctuation, capitalization, or spelling. • Uses a variety of sentence types. • Speaks somewhat clearly, using effective volume and intonation.	• Demonstrated good participation and decision making with few distractions. • Planning and used its time acceptably. • Demonstrated ability to negotiate opinions and compromise with little aggression or unfairness.
2	• Addresses only parts of the writing task. • Demonstrates little understanding of purpose and audience. • Maintains an inconsistent point of view, focus, and/or organizational structure, which may include ineffective or awkward transitions that do not unify important ideas. • Suggests a central idea with limited facts, details, and/or explanations.	• Demonstrates that the topic was minimally researched. • Uses a mix of relevant and irrelevant information. • Presents the topic with some factual errors and leaves some aspects unexplored. • Reaches conclusions that do not stem from evidence presented in the project.	• Contains several errors in grammar, punctuation, capitalization, or spelling. These errors may interfere with the reader's understanding of the writing. • Uses little variety in sentence types. • Speaks unclearly or too quickly. May interfere with the audience's understanding of the project.	• Demonstrated uneven participation or was often off-topic. Task distribution was lopsided. • Did not show a clear plan for the project, and did not use time well. • Allowed one or two opinions to dominate the activity, or had trouble reaching a fair consensus.
1	• Addresses only one part of the writing task. • Demonstrates no understanding of purpose and audience. • Lacks a point of view, focus, organizational structure, and transitions that unify important ideas. • Lacks a central idea but may contain marginally related facts, details, and/or explanations.	• Demonstrates that the topic was poorly researched. • Does not discriminate relevant from irrelevant information. • Presents the topic incompletely, with many factual errors. • Did not reach conclusions.	• Contains serious errors in grammar, punctuation, capitalization, or spelling. These errors interfere with the reader's understanding of the writing. • Uses no sentence variety. • Speaks unclearly. The audience must struggle to understand the project.	• Demonstrated poor participation by the majority of the group. Tasks were completed by a small minority. • Failed to show planning or effective use of time. • Was dominated by a single voice, or allowed hostility to derail the project.

NAME _____ **PROJECT** _____

DATE _____

ORGANIZATION & FOCUS	CONTENT	ORAL/WRITTEN CONVENTIONS	GROUP PARTICIPATION

COMMENTS AND SUGGESTIONS

UNDERSTANDING YOUR SCORE

Organization: Your project should be clear, focused on a main idea, and organized. You should use details and facts to support your main idea.

Content: You should use strong research skills. Your project should be thorough and accurate.

Oral/Written Conventions: For writing projects, you should use good composition, grammar, punctuation, and spelling, with a good variety of sentence types. For oral projects, you should engage the class using good public speaking skills.

Group Participation: Your group should cooperate fairly and use its time well to plan, assign and revise the tasks involved in the project.

NAME _____ GROUP MEMBERS _____

_____
_____
_____

Use this worksheet to describe your project by finishing the sentences below.
For individual projects and writing assignments, use the "How I did" section.
For group projects, use both "How I did" and "How we did" sections.

The purpose of this project is to :

[   ]

Scoring Key =   **4** – extremely well
                3 – well
                2 – could have been better
                1 – not well at all

HOW I DID

I understood the purpose and requirements for this project...

I planned and organized my time and work...

This project showed clear organization that emphasized the central idea...

I supported my point with details and description...

I polished and revised this project...

I utilized correct grammar and good writing/speaking style...

Overall, this project met its purpose...

HOW WE DID

We divided up tasks...

We cooperated and listened to each other...

We talked through what we didn't understand...

We used all our time to make this project the best it could be...

Overall, as a group we worked together...

I contributed and cooperated with the team...

NAME _____

LIBRARY / MEDIA CENTER RESEARCH LOG

DUE DATE _____

What I Need to Find

Places I Know to Look

Brainstorm: Other Sources and Places to Look

I need to use:
- ☐ primary sources.
- ☐ secondary

WHAT I FOUND

Title/Author/Location (call # or URL)

	Book/Periodical	Website	Other	Primary Source	Secondary Source	Suggestion	Library Catalog	Browsing	Internet Search	Web link	Rate each source from 1 (low) to 4 (high) in the categories below
											helpful / relevant
_____	☐	☐	☐	☐	☐	☐	☐	☐	☐	☐	____ / ____
_____	☐	☐	☐	☐	☐	☐	☐	☐	☐	☐	____ / ____
_____	☐	☐	☐	☐	☐	☐	☐	☐	☐	☐	____ / ____
_____	☐	☐	☐	☐	☐	☐	☐	☐	☐	☐	____ / ____
_____	☐	☐	☐	☐	☐	☐	☐	☐	☐	☐	____ / ____
_____	☐	☐	☐	☐	☐	☐	☐	☐	☐	☐	____ / ____

How I Found it

GRAPHIC ORGANIZERS

GUIDELINES

Reproducibles of seven different graphic organizers are provided on the following pages. These give your students a variety of ways to sort and order all the information they are receiving in this course. Use the organizers for homework assignments, classroom activities, tests, small group projects, and as ways to help the students take notes as they read.

1. Determine which graphic organizers work best for the content you are teaching. Some are useful for identifying main ideas and details; others work better for making comparisons, and so on.
2. Graphic organizers help students focus on the central points of the lesson while leaving out irrelevant details.
3. Use graphic organizers to give a visual picture of the key ideas you are teaching.
4. Graphic organizers can help students recall important information. Suggest students use them to study for tests.
5. Graphic organizers provide a visual way to show the connections between different content areas.
6. Graphic organizers can enliven traditional lesson plans and encourage greater interactivity within the classroom.
7. Apply graphic organizers to give students a concise, visual way to break down complex ideas.
8. Encourage students to use graphic organizers to identify patterns and clarify their ideas.
9. Graphic organizers stimulate creative thinking in the classroom, in small groups, and for the individual student.
10. Help students determine which graphic organizers work best for their purposes, and encourage them to use graphic organizers collaboratively whenever they can.
11. Help students customize graphic organizers as particular exercises dictate: e.g., more or fewer boxes, lines, or blanks than appear.

OUTLINE

MAIN IDEA: _____

_____

_____

    DETAIL: _____

    _____

    DETAIL: _____

    _____

    DETAIL: _____

    _____

MAIN IDEA: _____

_____

_____

    DETAIL: _____

    _____

    DETAIL: _____

    _____

    DETAIL: _____

    _____

Name _____ Date _____

MAIN IDEA MAP

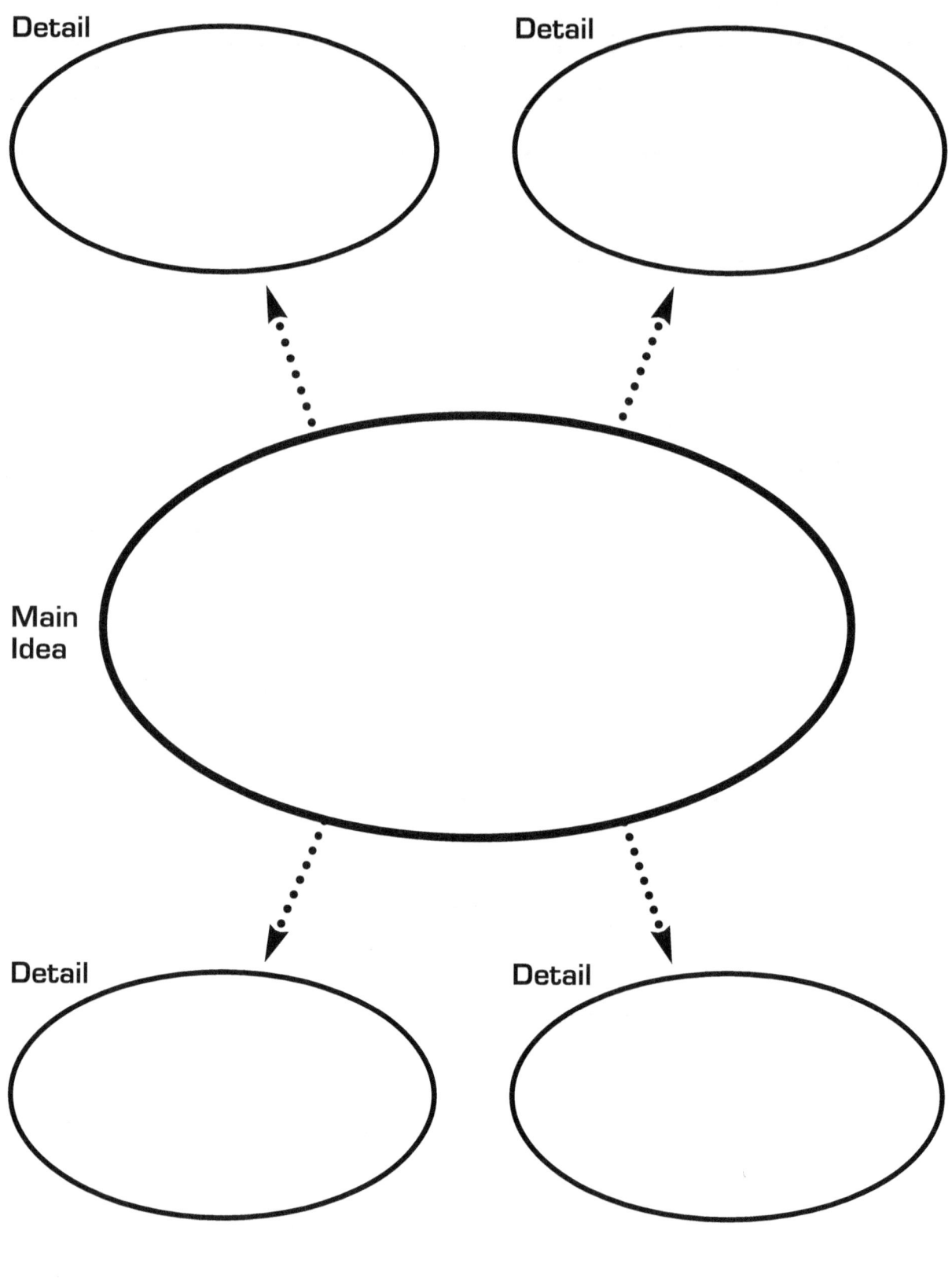

Detail

Detail

Main Idea

Detail

Detail

Name _____ Date _____

K-W-L CHART

K	W	L
What I Know	What I Want to Know	What I Learned

Name _____ Date _____

VENN DIAGRAM

Write differences in the circles. Write similarities where the circles overlap.

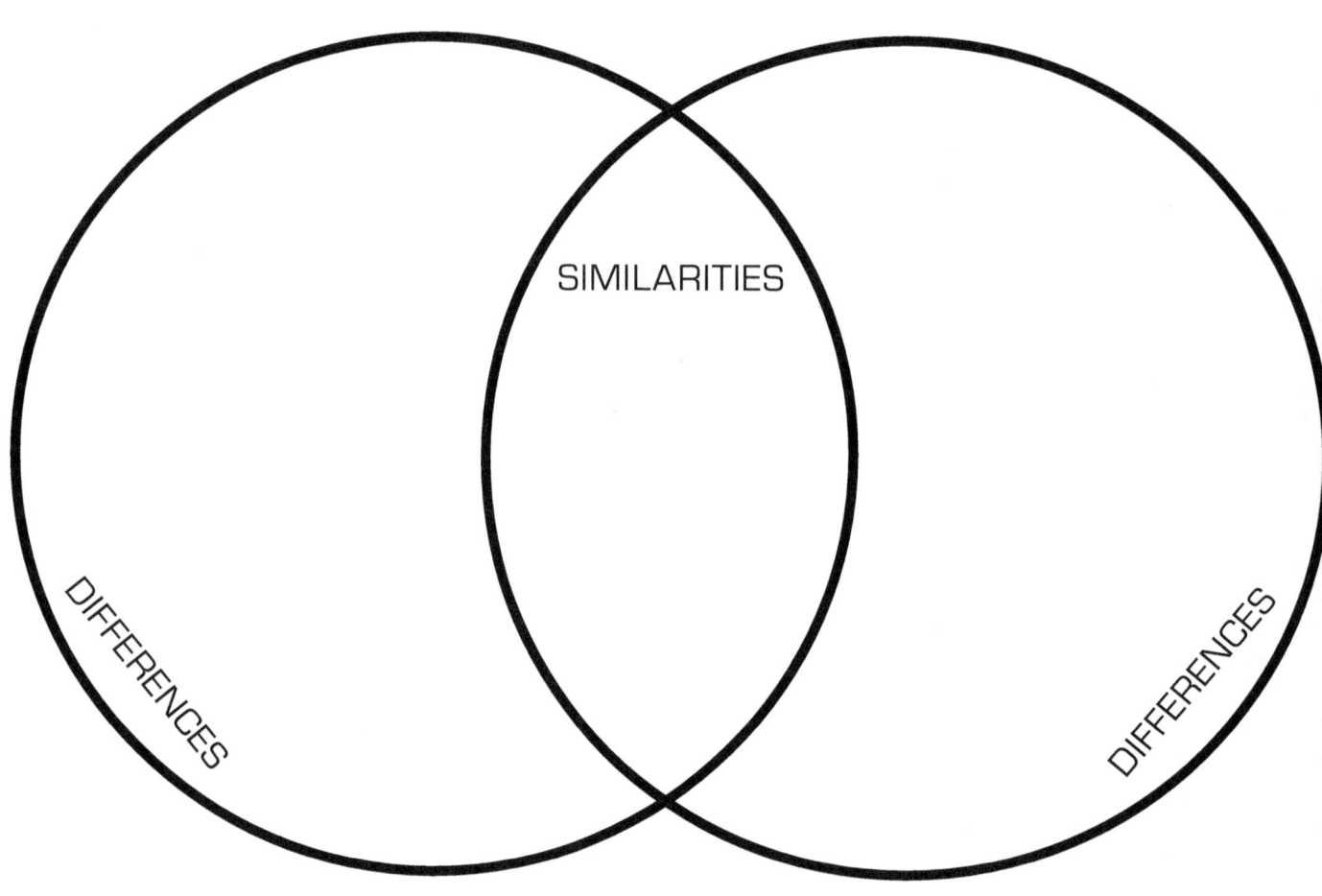

Name _____ Date _____

TIMELINE

DATE

EVENT Draw lines to connect the event to the correct year on the timeline.

Name _____ Date

SEQUENCE OF EVENTS CHART

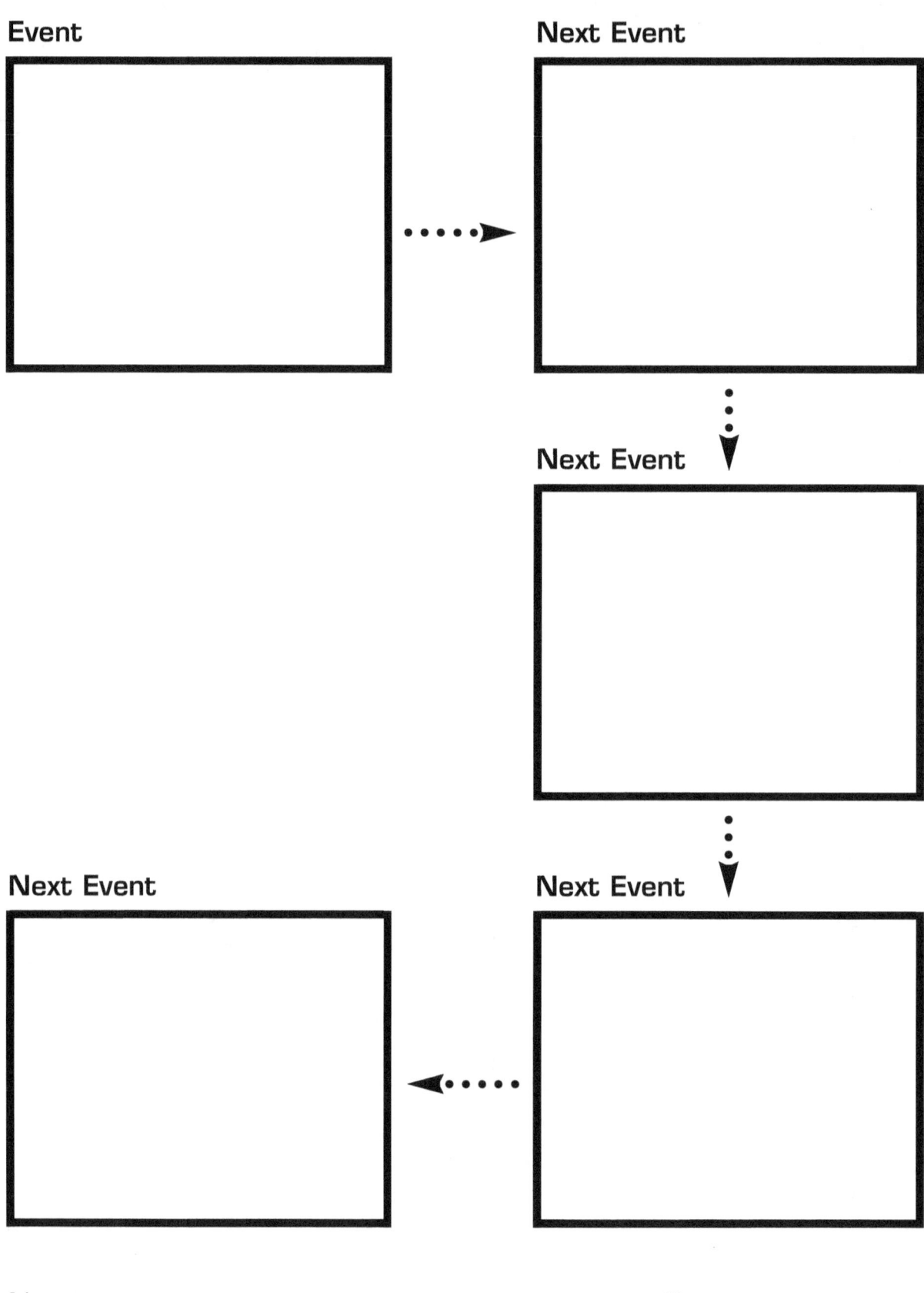

Name _____ Date _____

T-CHART

Cause | Effect

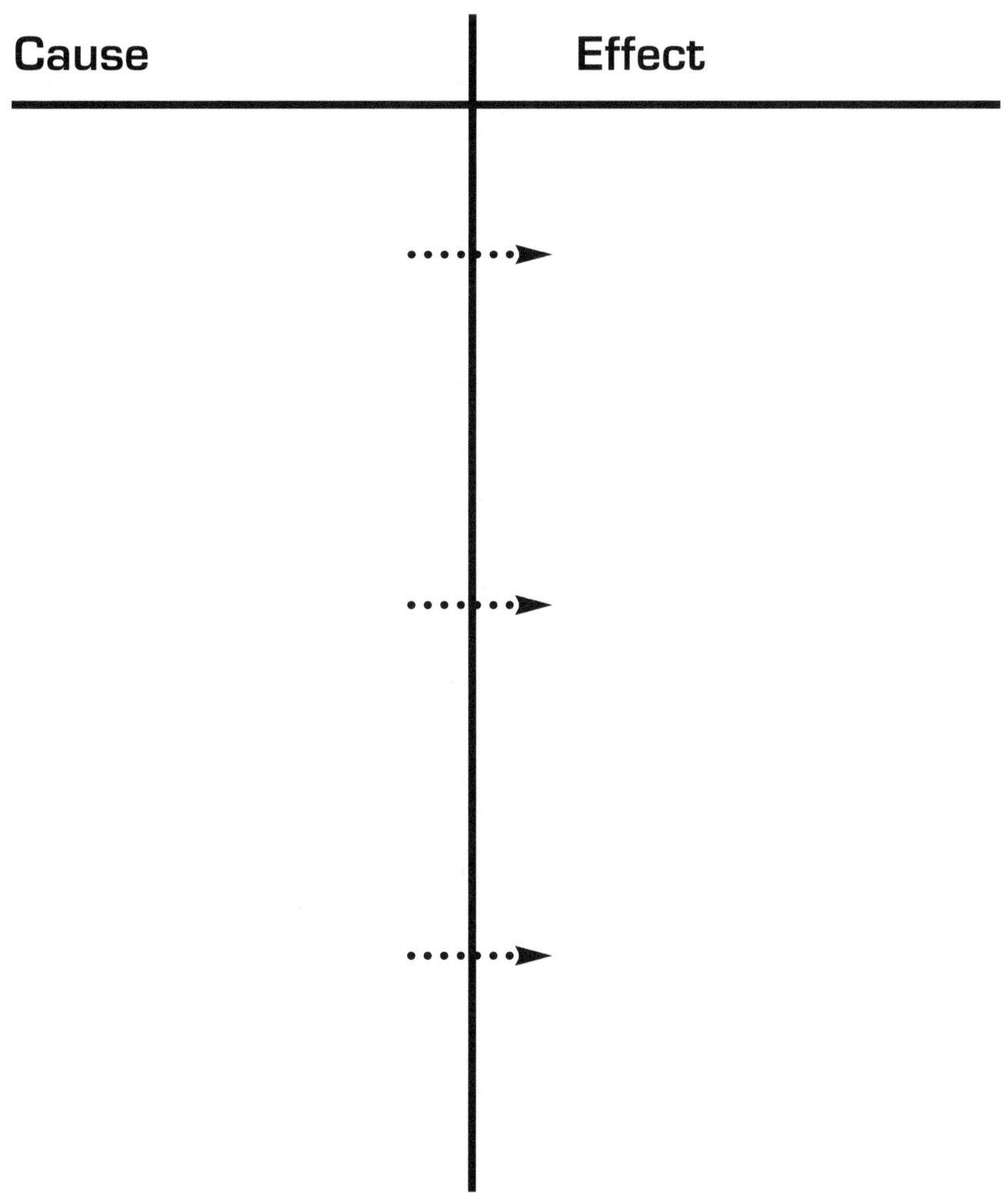

Name _____ Date _____

ANSWER KEY

CHAPTER 1

BLACKLINE MASTER 1
1. Hudson and Smith.
2. By boat because they traveled along the rivers.
3. Europe
4. Europe

BLACKLINE MASTER 2
1–3. Answers will vary
4. Students may mention that the speakers are both speaking highly and positively of the Native Americans.

CHAPTER TEST
A. **1.** c; **2.** a; **3.** d; **4.** a; **5.** b; **6.** c

B. **7.** He explored North America on at least two occasions and settled there. His was the first journey on which the English kept records.

8. Most students will describe Powhatan as a strong, dignified, intelligent, and humane leader.

9. Students may point out that Equiano was the son of an African king, gained his own freedom after ten years of slavery, not only became literate, but also wrote a best-seller, and contributed to the abolitionist cause.

C. Answers will vary but should highlight the main events and people such as Bartholomew Gosnold, Captain John Smith, Powhatan, and Olaudah Equiano.

CHAPTER 2

BLACKLINE MASTER 1
1. the seizing of ships and their cargo
2. piracy, a pirate
3. ton, laden, boards, apart
4. Answers will vary.

BLACKLINE MASTER 2
1. False; Wesley believes that the richer people get, the less religious they become.
2. True
3. False; Wesley believes that "the pride of life" is a bad quality for people to have.
4. False; Wesley presents no solution to the problem of maintaining "the essence of religion."

CHAPTER TEST
A. **1.** d; **2.** b; **3.** d; **4.** c; **5.** d; **6.** a

B. **7.** If merchants charged too much for their products, potential buyers would buy elsewhere.

8. The factory brought together in one place workers, raw materials, and machines.

C. Mercantilism is the economic system of increasing a country's wealth through trade and acquiring gold. Smith did not support mercantilism with its goal of gaining monopolies. He believed that the road to true wealth for countries lay in free trade.

CHAPTER 3

BLACKLINE MASTER 1
1. *devshirme,* or collection
2. Possible answer: The boys were taken from their families and reeducated to become loyal to the group in which they found themselves.
3. Students may write that the system was good because the education the boys received was excellent—better than they could have received any other way—and they had lots of opportunities for advancement. Or they may believe that taking children from their families is wrong no matter how well-treated they were.

BLACKLINE MASTER 2
1. People in England frequently died from smallpox, her brother included. She herself had scars from the disease.
2. People are exposed to small amounts of smallpox virus by scratching their skin and inserting a bit of liquid, become slightly ill, and develop an immunity to the disease.
3. *Possible answer:* She was not a scientist or doctor; she could not prove the process was safe, and perhaps the English were not able to accept that the Turks had found a way to avoid smallpox when they themselves had not.
4. Students may write *yes* because the disease was so deadly or no because the procedure seemed so risky and unsanitary.

CHAPTER TEST
A. **1.** b; **2.** c; **3.** d; **4.** b; **5.** b; **6.** d

B. **7.** He resisted the Ottoman Turks who were trying to take his castle 24 times.

8. This would give them respect for books especially the Quran.

9. He incorporated the combination of dome and tower of Muslim architecture in his own work.

C. Answers will vary but should include information about the training and education the pages received.

CHAPTER 4

BLACKLINE MASTER 1
1. Himalayas
2. Kandahar, Lahore, Allahabad, and Calcutta
3. Goa
4. Bombay

BLACKLINE MASTER 2
1. It was probably intended to inspire awe and impress viewers with the power and riches of the Mughal Empire.
2. *Possible answer:* The forty days of drumming.
3. *Possible answer:* The state must be prosperous, powerful, and technologically sophisticated enough to produce brocades and embroidered carpets.
4. Most students will believe that Jahangir was pleased with his coronation because he decided how it would be celebrated.

CHAPTER TEST
A. **1.** d; **2.** d; **3.** c; **4.** b; **5.** d; **6.** a

B. Elephants transported goods, helped with construction projects, and terrified enemies.

C. Answers will vary, but may include that Akbar was the greatest emperor because he was the most tolerant and governed fairly. The empire grew and thrived under his command and he was responsible for many lovely works of art and architecture.

CHAPTER 5

BLACKLINE MASTER 1
1. The inset shows the global route of Matteo Ricci; the large map shows only China.
2. Rome, Beijing
3. 900 miles (Majiao, Nanjing)
4. It was faster.

BLACKLINE MASTER 2
1. *Possible answer:* The ideal society would be fair, just, and orderly. In it everyone would know his or her place and respect the status of others.
2. Answers will vary.
3. Students will say it is familiar because it is nearly identical to the Golden Rule or the Biblical commandment.
4. Answers will vary.

ANSWER KEY

CHAPTER TEST

A. 1. b; **2.** b; **3.** d; **4.** d; **5.** c; **6.** d

B. 7. a ship from the Netherlands that capsized on its way back home from China on December 18, 1751

8. It tried to establish a demand for a new kind of product rather than merely meet existing demands.

C. Answers will vary but should include that he hung a picture of the Virgin Mary and the Baby Jesus and put astronomical instruments, clocks, and maps around his home so that the Chinese would be curious about these things and ask questions, providing an opportunity for him to talk about Christianity.

CHAPTER 6
BLACKLINE MASTER 1

1. *Possible answer:* No, he probably still believed that the earth revolved around the sun, but he was so frightened of the Inquisition he agreed to sign the confession.
2. *Possible answer:* They regarded Galileo's ideas as heresy, a sin against Catholic beliefs because the Bible seemed to contradict Galileo's ideas.

BLACKLINE MASTER 2

1. He uses figurative language when he describes Copernicus as abolishing circles, breaking solid skies, and taking the earth away from and putting the sun at the center of the universe.
2. *Possible answer:* He was excited and approving. His language expresses excitement and he writes that the sun "had a far better title to the honor" of being the center of the universe.
3. The planets and sun had been thought to revolve in perfect circles around the earth; and the sky had been thought to be solid rather than a gas.
4. *Possible answer:* Copernicus's idea of a sun-centered universe rightly revolutionized astronomy.

CHAPTER TEST

A. 1. d; **2.** a; **3.** a; **4.** b; **5.** b; **6.** d

B. Answers will vary but should express an understanding that Kepler used mathematics to confirm Copernicus's theories.

C. Answers will vary but should mention the scientific contributions of Ptolemy, Copernicus, Galileo, and Kepler.

CHAPTER 7
BLACKLINE MASTER 1

1. *Possible answers:* passivity; conformity, laziness, timidity.
2. *Possible answer:* He wanted people to use their own minds rather than relying on what others told them. Many students will feel that Kant's essay was persuasive because of the eloquence of his language.
3. *Possible answer:* It is easy to rely on experts and follow conventional wisdom, but difficult and threatening to think for oneself.

BLACKLINE MASTER 2

1. Gases themselves can't be observed directly, so their effects must be studied.
2. *Possible answer:* If the gas were the one Priestley expected, the mouse would soon die.
3. The mouse lasted for an hour in the glass and revived when he removed it. Priestley concluded that he had discovered a new gas, which came to be known as oxygen.
4. Yes, Priestley conducted an experiment to test a hypothesis. It was a simple, well-designed experiment that others could easily repeat to check his results and the conclusions he drew from them.

CHAPTER TEST

A. 1. c; **2.** d; **3.** b; **4.** b; **5.** d; **6.** a

B. 7. They thought they could only trust what they could see with their own eyes.

8. A Mercator map was a more precise and readable way to show a curved world on a flat surface. It distorted the area around the poles so that the north-south meridians remained parallel. It simplified navigation and revolutionized map making.

C. Answers will vary but should include that Newton lived a mostly solitary life and spent a lot of time thinking about scientific issues. He used the scientific method. He is also well-known for using an apple to describe the effects of gravity.

CHAPTER 8
BLACKLINE MASTER 1

1. *Possible answer:* Most people were only familiar with monarchies; the idea of a republic was new to them.
2. *Possible answer:* The people decide on representatives who make the laws, so the people actually rule, but then they must be subjects and follow the laws.
3. *Possible answer:* the people must elect the leaders of democracies, so the leaders risk losing power if they are unfair. Despotic forms of government rule by force, so they can act any way they want.

BLACKLINE MASTER 2

1. *Possible answer:* Voltaire says that the only goal of religion is "to keep mankind in order" so he seems to think that religion limits people's freedom. He believes that people should choose religion freely and not be forced into it.
2. Answers will vary.

CHAPTER TEST

A. 1. d; **2.** c; **3.** d; **4.** d; **5.** a; **6.** c

B. *Possible answer:* The first phrase means that the power of the monarchy comes from God and so it cannot be taken away by people. The second refers to governmental power being shared by executive, legislative, and judicial branches of government. The three thinkers would likely disagree with the idea expressed in the first phrase, but would agree with the second.

C. Answers will vary but may include that all three were writers who criticized the government. Voltaire and Diderot went to jail for their ideas. Voltaire and Montesquieu found a way of writing anonymously to avoid getting into more trouble. Voltaire's father wanted him to become a lawyer, Montesquieu was a lawyer.

CHAPTER 9
BLACKLINE MASTER 1

1. the padding used between delicate plates
2. Women are not considered important but they are the ones who keep everything together.
3. Women should not be treated poorly just because they always have been.
4. Both women discuss the poor treatment of women and yet the importance of women in society. They believe that the poor treatment of women should change.

BLACKLINE MASTER 2

1. a companion who can comfort and counsel him and think with a mind of her own
2. More says that society would prefer that women focus only on taking care of their families and not contributing intellectually.
3. to be educated and to be able to think for herself

CHAPTER TEST

A. 1. d; **2.** a; **3.** d; **4.** a; **5.** b

B. Answers will vary but should explain that Wollstonecraft is saying that women are wasting their lives trying to do what society tells them rather than using their brains that are capable of helping them accomplish more important things.

C. Answers will vary but should include that the salons were a place for people to gather to discuss philosophical and intellectual issues. Some of the accomplishments that came about through the salons, include creating a place for men and women to discuss important issues together, the creation of the *Encyclopedie*, and a new way of thinking about women's role in society.

AN AGE OF SCIENCE & REVOLUTIONS, 1600–1800

ANSWER KEY

CHAPTER 10
BLACKLINE MASTER 1
1. to practice their religion or hold religions services
2. to leave the kingdom and all territories of France
3. They were to be baptized as Catholics or their parents would be fined.
4. Answers will vary.

BLACKLINE MASTER 2
Answers will vary.

CHAPTER TEST
A. **1.** a; **2.** c; **3.** a; **4.** b; **5.** d

B. **6.** Charles I had closed down Parliament when it held back money and did not impose the taxes he wanted placed. This angered the Parliament, which eventually refused to close down. Although they did not want to execute the king, they eventually agreed when Cromwell fought for it.

7. Locke's ideas about the relationship between the government and the people are the foundation of the U.S. Declaration of Independence. American revolutionaries felt that the king of England was violating their rights base don these ideas.

C. Answers will vary but should mention the ideas described in *The Laws of War and Peace*, "natural laws," "the rights of war," and "just war."

WRAP-UP TEST
1. Students' paragraphs should note that among other differences, the goal of Gosnold's first voyage was to acquire trade goods to turn a profit on his return to England and that the goal of his second journey was to set up a colony in the New World.
2. Paragraphs should mention the following ideas: that trade benefits both buyers and sellers, that trade should be open, and that competition (the "Invisible Hand") prevents exploitation.
3. Paragraphs should note the coercive nature of the *devshirme* system in which non-Muslims were taken from their families to be educated. Particularly smart boys received excellent practical educations at the Imperial Palace School which prepared them for professions such as secretary, minister of state, and military commander; the Ottoman Empire benefited from such professionally trained administrators because its government was administered efficiently and fairly.
4. Students should mention both the symbolic and practical benefits of elephants, which were used for building projects and warfare and celebrated in art and literature.
5. Paragraphs should note that the Chinese belief that non-Chinese were barbarians prevented them from being open to new religious ideas. The complexity of Chinese society and its ancient philosophical and religious ideas also made conversion difficult.
6. Paragraphs should emphasize the importance of direct observation and compilation of data, as well as the willingness of Copernicus, Galileo, and Kepler to go against accepted Church doctrine in their theories of a sun-centered system.
7. Students' paragraphs should demonstrate an understanding that the scientific method in which nothing is assumed to be true but must be tested was the true revolution. Removing preconceived notions and bias let people look at the world more clearly and learn about it more accurately.
8. Students should explain that to Voltaire religious beliefs were transactions between individuals and God rather than being mediated by the church or kings. Paragraphs should demonstrate an understanding of the revolutionary effects of such an understanding.
9. Paragraphs should note Wollstonecraft's belief in the equal abilities of men and women, the goal of education being women's independence, and the benefits to both men and women of women's freedom.
10. Paragraphs should cite Locke's opposition to the idea that rulers held their position by divine right and in favor of universal freedom of religion. Though people have to give up certain freedoms to live together in a civil society according to Locke, he believed that they should never have to give up religious freedom.

ANSWERS FOR THE STUDENT STUDY GUIDE
CHAPTER 1

Causes and Effects
1. The natives drew a chalk map for Gosnold and his party to help them navigate their way south.
2. The food supply was running low and would not last through the winter. The sailors had heard that many colonists had starved there.
3. Many of the original settlers died from disease and hardship, and the Native Americans suffered a vast destruction from the spread of diseases they were not used to.
4. The colonists needed a workforce to help grow crops.

Cast of Characters
Captain Bartholomew Gosnold was an English explorer who discovered the coast of Maine in 1602. He gave Cape Cod its name.

Captain John Smith led the settlement at Jamestown. He was captured by the Indians and held captive for four weeks before he was released unharmed.

Powhatan was the Native American leader who pointed out the advantages to both the settlers and the Native Americans of peaceful cooperation.

Olaudah Equiano was the author of *The Interesting Narrative of the Life of Olaudah Equiano*, which told the story of his capture and enslavement in Africa and the horrific experience of coming over on a slave ship.

Word Bank
1. peninsula
2. monopoly
3. maneuver
4. alliances
5. consolidate

Word Play
countenance; synonyms could include *look, expression, visage, face, demeanor*

Working with Primary Sources
Percy came over from Europe to settle Jamestown. He saw a Native American chief with a bow and arrow, smoking a pipe. The chief asked why Percy and the rest of the settlers were there and told him he wanted them to go away. The settlers told the Indians that they came in peace and the Indians eventually let them enter their land without a struggle.

Making Inferences
1. Yes, because he knew how to write and his language is fairly sophisticated.
2. No, because he did not call them Indians or Native Americans, but could only describe their physical appearance. The Native Americans did not know why the settlers were there and the settlers had to justify themselves. They obviously had not seen each other before.
3. At first he felt hostile and defensive towards the chief, because he described the chief's speech as a "bold uttering" as if the chief did not have the right to say what he did. In the end, however, his feelings had changed to feelings of acceptance and tolerance because he admitted that the chief let them come onto the land without an argument.

Critical Thinking
Students should draw a Venn diagram with Captain Bartholomew Gosnold in one circle and Olaudah Equiano in another circle.

The men were similar because both traveled to new worlds, both experienced hardship in their travels, and neither saw their home country ever again. They were different because Gosnold came of his own free will and Equiano was kidnapped and brought over; Gosnold was the captain and then second-in-command of his ship while Equiano was crammed into the cargo hold with hundreds of other slaves; Gosnold could choose where he wanted to go and Equiano had to go wherever he was taken; and Gosnold was able to work because he chose to do so, while Equiano was forced to work.

All Over the Map
a) cotton, sugar, tobacco, molasses, rum, fish, iron
b) manufactured goods
c) flour, fish, meat, lumber
d) sugar, molasses, fruit, wood
e) rum, iron
f) slaves, gold
g) slaves, molasses
h) rice, fish, meat
i) horses, guns, manufactured goods
1. Charles Town, Philadelphia, New York, Boston, London, Lisbon
2. Answers will vary. One example: Slaves are the labor force needed to cut sugar cane in the West Indies, which is processed into molasses. The molasses is taken to cities in the British colonies, where it is made into rum. From there it goes across the Atlantic to England. England uses raw materials such as iron and cotton to make manufactured goods such as guns and clothing, which are then traded for more raw materials.
3. the middle passage

ANSWER KEY

CHAPTER 2

Cast of Characters
Antonio De Ulloa was a naval officer who was sent on an expedition by King Philip V of Spain to measure a segment of the meridian at the equator. While on the expedition, he recorded his observations about life in Peru.

Adam Smith was a brilliant economist who wrote The Wealth of Nations, which outlined how to make a society work economically.

John Wesley was a preacher in the Church of England in the early 1700s. He founded Methodism and believed that wealth was a threat to religion.

Word Bank
1. frugal 2. invincible 3. methodical 4. fleet 5. quotas

Word Play
Answers will vary.
Sample response: The player exhorted his team to pass him the ball, but the team members ignored him; Check students' sentences.

With a Parent or Partner
2. verb; meditate 3. both noun and verb in current form 4. noun; reveal

Critical Thinking
Answers will vary.
1. Cause: The Dutch and English fought for control of the English Channel and the shipping lanes that were part of it. Effect: The English ships kept out of range and defeated the Spanish ships.
2. Cause: Poor working conditions and brutal masters.
3. Effect: Piracy broke out and nations had to maintain naval fleets to protect their ships.
4. Cause: King Philip V of Spain sent Antonio De Ulloa on an expedition to measure part of the meridian in Peru.
5. Cause: Lots of available gold. Effect: Nobles had to sell their estates, and farmers working on those estates had nowhere to go.

Working with Primary Sources
Answers will vary.
Sample response to rephrasing: The division of labor came about naturally because human beings have an internal need to exchange one thing for another in order to further their own lives with the necessary materials and goods.

Making Inferences
Answers will vary.
1. Adam Smith was a brilliant economist who was able to understand how an economically perfect society would run.
2. Adam Smith must have been a very thoughtful individual based on the economic theories that he described in The Wealth of Nations.
3. Because Adam Smith was always so deep in his thoughts, he stumbled when he walked and must have looked very bizarre.

All Over the Map
1. From Europe to the East Indies
2. a) about 3,500 miles
   b) about 12,000 miles
   c) about 2,750 miles
3. a) going straight across the Indian Ocean
   b) going along the east coast of Africa and over to India
4. So they could do trade with the cities on the east coast of Africa and on the coast of India; also this would be safer than voyaging across open ocean, and ships would always be close to food and water on land.

CHAPTER 3

Cast of Characters
Kochu Bey was an Albanian or Macedonian scholar who was recruited as a young boy to serve in the Ottoman Empire. He eventually became Grand Vizier in the early 17th century.

Lufti Pasha was an Albanian or Macedonian scholar who was recruited as a young boy to serve in the Ottoman Empire. He eventually became Grand Vizier in the mid-16th century.

Albert Bobovi was a Polish page who was captured and enslaved in the royal Palace. After his release he revealed everything he knew about palace life and about being a page.

Suleiman was a highly-praised sultan of the Ottoman Empire. He tried to be just to all, was very well-educated, and began a series of building projects that gave the empire its distinctive style.

Sinan I was a brilliant architect who was hired by Suleiman to give the Ottoman Empire its distinctive architectural style. Studied by architects all over the world, Sinan's mosques were the inspiration for St. Paul's Cathedral in London.

Word Bank
1. converted
2. indispensable
3. niche
4. just
5. mosque
6. provinces
7. bazaars

Word Play
Answers will vary.
Sample response: In the past, only members of the elite classes were allowed to go to school to get an education; Check students' sentences.

Critical Thinking
Answers will vary slightly.
1. The boy was taken from his family.
2. The boy had a physical examination.
3. The boy had an intelligence test.
4. Depending on test results, the boy was sent to a family, the army, or the palace school.
5. The boy became a soldier, entered royal service, or held some other skilled job.

Working with Primary Sources
Answers will vary.
Students should point out his intelligence, his positive view of palace life, and his rise to a high position.

All Over the Map
Check students' work against map on p. 46
a) Paris
d) Samarkand
g) Athens
3. Mediterranean Sea, Black Sea, Persian Gulf, Red Sea
4. Draw circle to include the Balkan Peninsula

CHAPTER 4

Cast of Characters
Babur was the founder and leader of the Mughal Empire. In 1523, Babur succeeded in moving the Dynasty south into India.

Akbar was the father of Jahangir who rebelled against him. Akbar put together an army to travel to Agra to put down his son's defiance. He ended up fighting with his son for four years until Jahangir eventually took over the empire.

Jahangir was the son of Akbar. He was very rebellious, had a drinking problem, and liked to condemn convicts to die by elephant crushing. He also wrote poetry and loved music. He could be cruel or exceedingly fair and gentle.

Nur Jahan was the 20th wife of Jahangir. She took control of many court functions upon her marriage to Jahangir, and strongly supported artists, poets, and musicians.

Shah Jahan was Jahangir's son. He built both the Peacock Throne and the Taj Mahal. He was a steadier ruler than his father and helped increase the wealth of the empire dramatically.

Mumtaz Mahal was the niece of Nur Jahan and the wife of Shah Jahan. She died in her late 30s after giving birth to her 14th child.

Aurangzeb was the son of Shah Jahan and Mumtaz Mahal, who took the empire by force. He killed or subdued his brothers, and held his father prisoner. He ruled the empire from 1658 to 1707.

Word Bank
1. sibling
2. seclusion
3. revenue
4. intimidating
5. outpost
6. caste
7. expedition

Word Play
Answers will vary.
Synonym: moveable
Antonym: fixed

Critical Thinking
1. c 2. g 3. a 4. h 5. d 6. b, e 7. f

Working with Primary Sources
Students should be able to point out, among other things, jewels such as diamonds, rubies, pearls, the "soaring" canopy; the lavish use of gold in different places, sapphire and gold peacocks over the head of the emperor.

ANSWER KEY

Making Inferences
Answers will vary.
Students may suggest that he wanted to demonstrate his wealth and power to his people and especially to potential enemies and traders from other countries.

In Your Own Words
Answers will vary.
Students might talk about the coaches, doolees, and palanqueeenes, the animals in the parade, the cloth and jewels, all of the flags, the streamers, and the number of people.

All Over the Map
Questions **1**, **2**, and **4**: check students' work against map on page 61
3. Allahabad
5. They were not strong enough to assert their authority over local princes, who created their own armies and collected their own taxes. Also, British officials through the East India Company were gaining more administrative control over Indian territories and affairs.

CHAPTER 5

Cast of Characters
Matteo Ricci was an Italian Jesuit and Chinese scholar who traveled to China with the aim of converting the Chinese to Christianity. In the process he introduced them to maps and geography, mathematics, and other forms of science, bridging the gap between Westerners and the Chinese.
Confucius was a Chinese philosopher who lived in the 6th century. His sayings were collected in a volume known as the Analects. The Chinese believed that studying this text was the path to scholarly enlightenment.
Emperor Zhu Yizhun ruled China when Ricci arrived in Beijing. He was a recluse who ignored his duties as Emporer. Ricci tried many times to meet him but the closest he ever got was fixing the Emperor's clock.
Cornelius Pronk was a Dutch painter who created porcelain in China from European designs. The "Parasol Ladies" is one of his most popular works.

Word Bank
1. reclusive
2. motives
3. porcelain
4. barbarians
5. audience
6. provisions

Word Play
Answers may vary.
Sample response: After hitting a large iceberg, the ship capsized, killing all of its passengers and crew.

Critical Thinking
Answers will vary.
Likenesses: valued study and scholarship; Western: explored the world, experimented, inquired; Chinese: studied philosophers, memorized texts, used scholarship to gain political power

Working with Primary Sources
Answers will vary.

Point of View
Answers will vary.
Sample response: Ricci probably just thought of the Chinese as souls to convert to Christianity at first. But he became impressed with Chinese culture and language as shown by his many years of study, his meetings with Chinese scholars, and his decision to dress like an upper-class Chinese.

All Over the Map
1. One is an inset map, to show how Ricci reached China from Europe. The larger map of China actually shows a smaller area, and it shows the cities in China at the time of Ricci's mission
2. Majiao and Guangzhou
3. Beijing
4. He sailed west through the Mediterranean, then around Africa, then north east across the Indian ocean, along the Indian coast and through southeast Asia to the Chinese coast.

CHAPTER 6

Cast of Characters/Access
Ptolemy was a Greek astronomer who spent his life trying to explain the movement of the sun, earth and stars. He concluded that the earth was the center of the universe and everything else moved in a circle around it.
Ibn al-Haytham was a Muslim scholar who concluded that Ptolemy's Almagest was wrong. He believed that a true model for the movement of the five planets had yet to be discovered.
Nicolaus Copernicus was a Polish doctor who believed that the sun was the center of the universe. He came up with a set of principles for a new system of astronomy, which he published as the Little Commentary.
Galileo Galilei was an astronomer who thought that people should believe in the reasoned conclusions stemming from observation over what the Bible told people to believe. His belief in a sun-centered universe got him into trouble with the Church, and as the result of his being tried as a heretic, he was forced to sign a confession claiming that his observations were false and that he only believed in what the Church had already established.
Tycho Brahe was a Danish man whose observations of astronomical phenomenon led to the most accurate data available in the world.
Johannes Kepler was a mathematical genius, who interpreted Brahe's data and came up with three astronomical laws governing the way the planets move in the universe.

Word Bank
1. fathom
2. orbit
3. heresy
4. exile
5. vengeance

Word Play
Answers will vary. Check students' sentences.
Sample response: Most people in the 1500s believed that the sun rotated around the earth.

Critical Thinking
6. 3, 8, 2, 5, 4, 1, 7, 6

Working with Primary Sources
Answers will vary.
1. apostolic: relating to the pope as holding spiritual authority.
   unfeigned: genuine.
   abjure: renounce under oath.
   assert: affirm.
2. *Sample answer:* I, Galileo, believe in everything the Church teaches, apologize for saying that the sun is the center of the universe, and promise I will never say or write anything like this again.
3. *Sample answer:* By demonstrating how the heavens worked through such an ingenious system, Kepler probably believed he was celebrating God who created it.

In Your Own Words
Answers will vary.
Students should refer to ideas such as: religion and science do not have to be mutually exclusive; that the Inquisition should review Galileo's data and observations; that people would not advance their knowledge if they relied only on what people had always said in the past. Speaking from the lawyer's perspective to the Inquisition, students' statements might praise religion and the church for enabling Galileo to make the observations he did with the tools he used, pointing out that God would not have allowed this to happen if he didn't want the truth to be known.

CHAPTER 7

Cast of Characters
Marcello Malpighi was an Italian physician who made observations about the world using a microscope. He tested and proved a theory that blood moves through the body by a pump (the heart), going out through the arteries and back in through the veins.
William Harvey was a British physician who believed that blood circulated through the body several times a day. He discovered that the heart was like a pump, but could not figure out how old blood was "refreshed" so that it could circulate through the body again.
Gerhard Kremer was a Flemish mapmaker who developed a more precise and user-friendly way to represent a curved world on the flat surface of a map. His map design is known today as the Mercator projection.
René Descartes was a French mathematician who created the philosophy "I think, therefore I am." Though he did exceptional work in mathematics, physics, and philosophy, he was sickly from a young age and died when he was only 53 years old.

ANSWER KEY

Francis Bacon was an Englishman who was influential in the way we think about science. He published *The New Organon* in order to describe his intellectual philosophy, and came up with four kinds of biases, or "idols" that need to be considered when conducting scientific experiments.

Isaac Newton is said to be one of the greatest scientists of all time. He believed the universe could be explained by mathematics and eventually created calculus in order to explain motion in objects. He discovered gravity and did not believe in a conflict between science and religion.

Joseph Priestley was an English scientist who laid the foundation for what we now call chemistry. He is best known for his experiments with gases, in particular, his discovery of oxygen.

Word Bank
1. infinite
2. contemplative
3. infinitesimal
4. bias
5. erratically

Word Play
Students might draw a circle with vertical lines passing through both the top and bottom of the circle, to show meridian lines.

Cause and Effect
Answers will vary.
Possible causes and effects that students might list include:

The telescope was invented = Galileo made new discoveries about the universe

The microscope was invented = Malpighi discovered how blood flows through the body

New techniques were used in mapmaking = Mercator created the Mercator projection, which made it easier to read maps

An apple fell to the ground = Newton discovered the laws of gravity

Working with Primary Sources
1. He is respectful and impressed by Isaac's dedication to science.
2. Answers will vary. *Possible answers:* intense devotion to the subject; perseverance; single-mindedness and focus; precision and accuracy

Writing
Answers will vary.
A possible answer might be:

I do not believe that Kant and Descartes were correct that reason and reason alone is the only way to gain enlightenment. I believe that reason is the only way to establish something as a fact, however, people are enlightened by all kinds of observations and ideas about the unknown. Most of the population of the world subscribes to a particular religion, and these people are enlightened by that religion even though none of it can be proven as fact.

CHAPTER 8

Cast of Characters
François-Marie Arouet de Voltaire, born François-Marie Arouet, was a philosopher, novelist, and political essayist.

Baron de Montesquieu was a philosopher and writer who proposed the separation of the powers of government.

Dénis Diderot was a philosopher who organized and edited the French *Encyclopédie*.

Word Bank
1. censors
2. corruption
3. crusaders
4. random
5. despoiled
6. parliament
7. reform

Word Play
Synonym: slight
Antonym: obvious

Critical Thinking
Answers may vary.
1. Voltaire, Montesquieu, and Diderot were revolutionary in their ideas. They tried to push their boundaries in order to say what they thought was right. They believed that the truth should be brought to the people no matter what the cost. The Church and the government of France worked together to try to squelch the three men because their ideas strongly criticized both the government of France and the Church.
2. Students might suggest that the common people were affected the most by these new ideas because they are the group that was being held back by the government. They were not given an education, they were told what to believe, and they did not have the rights that money could buy royalty and the nobles. The new ideas gave them hope that they deserved to be treated as equals with the higher classes.

Who Wrote What?
1. b, fiction
2. c, nonfiction
3. a, nonfiction

Working with Primary Sources
Answers may vary.
1. *Sample response:* I agree that all topics are fair game for study. There is no reason why any topic should be off-limits, except to hide corruption and falsities. It is only through study that we can discover the truth about a topic, and that is something we should all strive for.
2. *Sample response:* Encyclopedia editors still want to record events and knowledge so that it is not lost, but they may not have as big of expectations for the masses reading their work. Now that the majority of people are given the chance for a basic education, it is not as crucial that the poorer classes read the encyclopedia in order to learn about various topics.
3. *Sample response:* In democracies, the people are, in a way, the rulers. However, just because they create the laws does not mean that they are allowed to do whatever they want. Laws are created so that order may be kept in the country. As long as what they are doing is not illegal, people in democracies can do and say as they please.

CHAPTER 9

Cast of Characters
Caroline Herschel was a German-born astronomer who was the first woman to discover a comet.

William Herschel was a German-born astronomer renowned for discovering the planet Uranus in 1781, among other astronomical accomplishments.

Madame Anne Thérèse de Lambert was a French marquess famous for hosting biweekly meetings of scholars, writers, and artists in her salon.

Jean-Jacques Rousseau was a French philosopher and author of *The Social Conract*.

Mary Wollstonecraft was a feminist author who wrote Vindication of the Rights of Women.

Marie Thérèse Geoffrin was the hostess of a salon that supported the Encyclopédie.

Hannah More, an English feminist, writer, and philanthropist.

Word Bank
1. comet
2. salon
3. typhus
4. Enlightenment

Word Play
Answers may vary.
Sample response: When people study astronomy, they are learning about the planets and stars that make up the universe.

Critical Thinking
1. Caroline Herschel's mother would not let her go to school so she stayed at home working as a maid. (d)
2. Caroline Herschel helped her brother make telescopes so she learned about astronomy. (a)
3. Aristocratic women hosted salons so intellectuals had a place to gather to discuss important issues of the day. (b)
5. Marie Thérèse Geoffrin had a limited education so the discussions in the salons were her only education. (e)
6. Many political leaders were against change and revolutionary actions so Mary Wollstonecraft wrote *A Vindication of the Rights of Man*. (c)

AN AGE OF SCIENCE & REVOLUTIONS, 1600–1800

ANSWER KEY

Working with Primary Sources
Answers will vary.
Sample response to the first quotation: The quotation means that it is unfair for men to assume that just because women have been held back by society in the past, things should remain that way in the future. Men should separate themselves from corrupt kings and others who have taken advantage of their position of power, by making reasonable and informed decisions. Unfair practices should not exist simply because it has always been that way.

Sample response to the second quotation: Women are seen as soft insignificant buffers, yet they keep everything together without breaking.

CHAPTER 10

Cast of Characters
Hugo Grotius was a Dutchman who believed rational inquiry could uncover a "natural law" for universal standards of human conduct.

King Charles I of England was an English king executed in 1649 after losing a power struggle with Parliament that sparked the English Civil War.

Oliver Cromwell was a British general who assumed the title of Lord Protector in 1653 after overthrowing Charles I in the English Civil War.

John Locke was an English philosopher who championed constitutional government.

Word Bank
Treason: The offense of attempting by overt acts to overthrow the government of the state to which the offender owes allegiance or to kill or personally injure the sovereign or the sovereign's family.

Sample sentence: The British soldier committed treason when he told the enemy army where they could find the king.

Critical Thinking
Fact: 3, 4, 6, 7
Opinion: 1, 2, 5, 8

Working with Primary Sources
Answers may vary.
1. c; **2.** a
Locke is referring to freedom of religion.

All Over the Map
Questions **1–3**: check against map on page 152

Write About It
Answers will vary, but they should include discussion about the fact that all the revolutions were expressions of the people's will against the authority of a king. The French Revolution was partly inspired by the American Revolution. The Glorious Revolution was different from the others in that there was no fighting. It became an inspiration for the U.S. Constitution, drafted after the American Revolution.

www.ingramcontent.com/pod-product-compliance
Lightning Source LLC
LaVergne TN
LVHW080250260326
834688LV00042BA/1209